Unlocking the Power of Matthew 5

for *Thirst* GOD

MIGUEL VALDIVIA

Pacific Press®
Publishing Association
Nampa, Idaho | www.pacificpress.com

Cover design by Gerald Lee Monks
Cover design resources from GettyImages.com
Inside design by Aaron Troia

The author assumes full responsibility for the accuracy of all facts and quotations as cited in this book.

Purchase additional copies of this book by calling toll-free 1-800-765-6955 or by visiting AdventistBookCenter.com.

Library of Congress Cataloging-in-Publication Data

Names: Valdivia, Miguel, 1958- author.
Title: Thirst for God : unlocking the power of Matthew 5 / Miguel A. Valdivia.
Description: Nampa, Idaho : Pacific Press Publishing Association, 2021. |
    Includes bibliographical references. | Summary: "Jesus' teachings on spiritual
    growth, drawn from the beatitudes in His sermon on the mount"— Provided
    by publisher.
Identifiers: LCCN 2021001233 (print) | LCCN 2021001234 (ebook) |
    ISBN 9780816367580 (paperback) | ISBN 9780816367597 (ebook)
Subjects: LCSH: Beatitudes—Criticism, interpretation, etc. |
    Spiritual formation—Christianity.
Classification: LCC BT382 .V27 2021 (print) | LCC BT382 (ebook) |
    DDC 248.4/82—dc23
LC record available at https://lccn.loc.gov/2021001233
LC ebook record available at https://lccn.loc.gov/2021001234

January 2021

Dedication

To Alan, Brian, and Cindy, the ABCs who have graced my life with joy and fulfillment. To Olga, my wonderful wife of many years and many joint prayers.

Endorsements for *Thirst for God*

In *Thirst for God*, my long-time friend, Miguel Valdivia, unlocks the power of the Beatitudes through personal stories and reflections that will move the reader to both prayer and action. The eight blessings from the Sermon on the Mount are a revolutionary call to being like God in a world that has no room for Him. If you're thirsty for a walk with God that goes deeper than surface religion, this book is your ticket to the blessed life.—Randy Maxwell, author, *If My People Pray*, and pastor, Renton Seventh-day Adventist Church.

In a time of pandemic, racial tension, economic crisis, and political divide, the followers of Jesus must take their cue, not from political leaders of any party, nor from the media, but from the heart of Jesus. As you read *Thirst for God* you will be able to see into His heart and into an infinite universe of blessings for people whom contemporary society may not always look up to, but whom Jesus calls blessed. Valdivia's insightful and practical gem will lead you to a daily life of blessing through the eyes of the One who loves you most, Jesus.—Jose Cortés Jr., associate ministerial director, Evangelism, North American Division of Seventh-day Adventists.

I was deeply moved by reading *Thirst for God*. The stories touched my heart and brought me closer to God. The biblical insight helped me to have a deeper appreciation for the Beatitudes. Even though I have read them many times, it was as if I were reading them for the first time. My heart was thrilled with the new insight I gained. If you want to move onto higher ground spiritually and appreciate in a new way the blessings that Jesus gives us when we follow Him, *Thirst for God* is a must read book for you.—S. Joseph Kidder, professor of pastoral theology and discipleship, Andrews University.

Insightful, creative, and relevant—Valdivia's *Thirst for God* offers a fresh approach to the timeless Beatitudes of Jesus found in Matthew's Gospel. Highlighting a reversal of values in light of the Cross, this book invites the reader to embark on a spiritual journey of total dependence on God. It beckons us to trust in Him not only in matters of eternal salvation but also in experiencing the kingdom of heaven and its many blessings through our relationships with God and fellow human beings here and now.—Elizabeth Viera Talbot, PhD, speaker/director of the Jesus 101 Biblical Institute (Jesus101.tv).

Contents

Introduction 7

A Change in Perspective 11

The Kingdom Mind 19

The Pain of Unworthiness 29

Sad for the Right Reasons 37

The Prayer of Humility 47

Thirst for God 57

Mercy, a Matter of the Heart 67

The Sin Problem 79

What It Means to Follow the Prince of Peace 89

The Price of Being Different 99

The Science of Spiritual Blessings 109

Conclusion: On My Back, Looking Up 119

Appendix 125

Throughout the Beatitudes there is an advancing line of Christian experience. Those who have felt their need of Christ, those who have mourned because of sin and have sat with Christ in the school of affliction, will learn meekness from the divine Teacher.

—Ellen G. White, *Thoughts From the Mount of Blessing*

Introduction

The thesis of the book you hold in your hands is that spiritual growth is possible. In fact, most people believe that there *should* be progress in the Christian experience. As we travel through time, those of us who consider ourselves spiritually minded generally expect to achieve growth and progressive success in our journey.

We believe that there should be a spiritual evolution—that we learn as we go, that our experiences are adding layers of spiritual sediment, slowly solidifying our character and softening our rough edges. In fact, this assurance of progress is what gives meaning and determination to what we choose to believe.

Over many years as a practicing pastor, supportive layperson, and Bible student, I have often heard some version of the question, "Will God really change me?" This question implies that we believe there is a process to salvation, that redemption involves a journey from point A to point B. It is based on the notion that we as humans are missing something—that our nature is lacking something that was lost and is worth recovering. And the gospel makes the universal invitation to engage in a spiritual journey with that objective in mind.

Ellen White's insightful Conflict of the Ages series bookends the story of human redemption with references to the origin of evil and the eventual restoration of harmony as the ultimate evidence of God's love. This cosmic restoration of creation and humanity also takes place in the microcosm of the human heart. Our spiritual journey should have an upward direction that results in achieving harmony with God.

Having admitted to this general truth, we must also acknowledge that our spiritual trajectory is seldom straight. Our experience can often be so challenging that a graph of our spiritual condition may look more like an EKG than an ascending line along an x-y axis. Life has a way of throwing rocks and boulders on our hiking path so that instead of a quiet, contemplative walk, we become immersed in dodging, hiding, and fighting for our existence.

Looking to better understand the *how* of spiritual progress, I'm inviting the reader to go back to the words of Jesus in His first major sermon on the nature of God's kingdom and the list of blessings in Matthew 5. I believe that beyond challenging the Jewish mind to understand the nature of His mission, Jesus may have been giving us clues about the progress He wants to enable in our lives.

I'm not alone in this thesis. Ellen White briefly alludes to the theme of spiritual progression in the list of Matthew 5. She wrote, "Throughout the Beatitudes there is *an advancing line of Christian experience*. Those who have felt their need of Christ, those who have mourned because of sin and have sat with Christ in the school of affliction, will learn meekness from the divine Teacher."[1] I also believe that there is tremendous power in understanding the dynamics contained in the spiritual progression of Matthew 5. You will notice that every chapter in this book includes a sample prayer and an invitation to create a personal list of spiritual goals in line with the teachings of Scripture. At the end of each chapter, you will find one or two "application" questions to encourage processing the concepts presented in the preceding pages.

Three major principles will guide our discovery: (1) We won't be seeking immediate rewards in our devotional response to what we learn from Scripture; rather, we will look to God to reveal His thoughts in this passage. (2) We will be open to entering into greater dependence on God and less dependence on ourselves. (3) We will allow for the possibility that the Spirit may lead us to a ministry response.

---

1. Ellen G. White, *Thoughts From the Mount of Blessing* (Oakland, CA: Pacific Press®, 1896), 13, 14; emphasis added.

Jesus saw that religion in His day had become increasingly rigid and self-serving. Defense of tradition and institutions was obscuring the values of God's kingdom. Human perspective was distancing itself from God's. His audience needed what they couldn't see yet. Their spiritual route needed recalculating; the templates they had built to understand God and religion were either faulty, imprecise, or ineffective.

—p. 15

Chapter 1

A Change in Perspective

I've struggled with poor eyesight most of my life. I was prescribed lenses when I was about eight years old. Today, without glasses, I'm what you would call legally blind. One side effect of having such poor sight and needing such a strong eyeglasses prescription is that I see everything around me a little smaller than it really is. For many years, I would see people and ask my wife, "Is that guy taller or shorter than me?"

Her answer would invariably be, "Much taller."

I'm glad I've had no physical confrontations with these "short" people around me all these years!

I mention this because perception is important. Perception is how we interpret the information we receive through our senses. Just think about how you relate to the world around you. When you go to a restaurant, you choose a certain dish based on expectations related to the way the food smells, looks, and tastes. Ice cream entices you with its texture, its flavor, and the way it melts in your mouth.

When we listen to someone singing a song, we recognize

the melody as well as the singer's voice and intonation. As the sounds reach our ears, our brain acknowledges and interprets them. Our brain will also decide whether these sounds are agreeable to our ears and whether we like or dislike the song.

Thus, our perception also includes how we respond to the information. We receive information through our senses, and we use that information to relate to our environment. Perception also allows us to make this information into something meaningful.

Right now, as you read these words, your brain is recognizing the shape of each letter. It distinguishes an *e* from an *a*. But it goes much further than that. You are interpreting groupings of letters and assigning meaning to each word. Our brain is even capable of interpreting whole words based on incomplete groupings of letters. Srsly, dn't stp rdng nw.

Those who have studied Hebrew realize that advanced readers don't need nor find vowels in everyday printed Hebrew such as newspapers or magazines. The three short vowels that tell seminary students how to pronounce a Hebrew word are missing everywhere but in biblical texts.

Psychologists have defined the science of human perception in much detail. One classic explanation is that through experience, the mind builds perceptual categories of objects. These categories emerge from basic interaction with the object and, in humans, via conceptual knowledge and naming. These perceptual (and, to a lesser extent, conceptual) categories serve as schema, or templates, and perception occurs via the process of matching sensory input patterns to perceptual templates.[1]

Our brain needs to build "templates" to facilitate its interpretation of the world around us. As we go about our lives, we are constantly (and unconsciously) organizing sensory information and then matching it to our previously collected knowledge. These templates, or molds, also shape our expectations. We recognize the rarity or impossibility of a truly black rose. We would also instinctively reject blue beans or purple tofu. Of course, this cataloging of impressions carries the immense risk of tainting our relationships with concepts (or people) that don't fit our templates.

The fact is that perception is the only means we have to interpret our surroundings. If our perception is off, our judgment and our opinions and our worldview will be off. My color-blind friends go through life with limitations that only others with similar afflictions can understand. One depends completely on his wife to choose what he wears every day. Another always asks for written reports instead of color-coded graphs because a color key does not mean much to him.

Perception is especially important when it comes to our psychological and spiritual makeup. How we perceive things and interpret them shapes our perspective. And perspective is generally defined as a particular attitude toward something—in the simplest of terms, a point of view, a frame of mind, or frame of reference.*

Jesus knew about the dangers of having the wrong perspective. All around Him, He saw men, women, and young people trapped in erroneous points of view. Their religion, based as it was on the wrong premises, simply did not work. The Bible says that Jesus felt compassion for them. "They were harassed and helpless, like sheep without a shepherd" (Matthew 9:36; compare Mark 6:34). Thus, He went up to a small mountain

---

* The study of human psychology recognizes five major perspectives: (1) biological, how our physical nature helps shape our thoughts and behavior; (2) psychodynamic, the connection between unconscious drives and early experiences and our thoughts; (3) behavioral, how external stimuli can influence our behavior; (4) cognitive, the role of emotions and expectations in coloring our understanding; (5) humanistic, the concept that every person makes choices wanting to improve their lives. (Saul A. McLeod, "Psychology Perspectives," Simply Psychology. updated 2013, https://www.simplypsychology.org/perspective.html.)

on the shores of the Sea of Galilee to tell them the truth about His Father.

Why climb a mountain? Let us think about mountains for a minute or two. In the Bible are many mentions of mountains: Mount Ararat, Mount Sinai, Mount Carmel, Mount Calvary. It could almost be argued that Bible history is told from mountaintops. Psalm 121 says,

I lift up my eyes to the mountains—
    where does my help come from?
My help comes from the LORD,
    the Maker of heaven and earth (verses 1, 2).

For some things, mountains are better than valleys. Armies like them better. They provide an advantage in battle and in reconnaissance. They give a better line of sight and add the help of gravity in throwing objects. When it comes to spiritual matters, mountains often inspire reverence and provide a setting for prayer and meditation.

By ascending a mountain, Jesus was calling His listeners to a higher plane of existence, because altitude brings a wider perspective. A song by the Heritage Singers talked about how you get a new point of view when you go for a balloon ride. When you are up high, everything changes. Large things become smaller, especially man-made things. Except, perhaps, for such large scale structures as the Great Wall of China or the Hoover Dam, if we go high enough, most of what human might has built degrades into minute groups of pixels in our retinas.

Our perspective dictates our life's journey. We develop wants and objectives based on our perception of what's important. In a materialistic society, we start equating possessions with achievement and well-being. We want to live large and be in charge. We build to exist. We buy to grow our self-worth. We feed our senses to feel alive, sometimes to our disappointment.

When my wife and I travel to Portland, Oregon, we often visit a mansion built by a newspaper magnate, Henry Pittock. It was completed in 1914. The impressive property features gardens and a panoramic view of the whole city. It is a veritable dream home with the latest technology for its day. Ironically, when you read the signs, you discover that the Pittocks spent years building their masterpiece, but after it was finished, they lived only four years to enjoy it.

We, too, often find that even achieving our dreams doesn't bring us lasting fulfillment. The new car smell fades promptly; the new position brings more stress than satisfaction; fame eats away at our peace of mind. We realize that we may be after the wrong kind of dreams. We come to understand that what we possess possesses us. We become slaves to what we crave. Our lives are as devoid of meaning as our garages are filled to the brim with our futile attempts at fulfillment.

Even our spiritual templates may be faulty. Jesus saw that religion in His day had become increasingly rigid and self-serving. Defense of tradition and institutions was obscuring the values of God's kingdom. Human perspective was distancing itself from God's. His audience needed what they couldn't see yet. Their spiritual route needed recalculating; the templates they had built to understand God and religion were either faulty, imprecise, or ineffective.

Their point of view needed to change; thus, Jesus led them to higher ground. There He sat down and spoke to them about the kingdom of heaven, what it meant to belong to that kingdom. Their perceptions needed retuning. Their frame of reference had to change before they could understand the kingdom.

You see, God's perspective is vastly different from ours. Everything about Him is beyond our comprehension. Our senses can't process the reality of an all-powerful Creator, of human-like hands shaping the universe, of infinite energy turning into matter. He stands above it all, and every human achievement, every ambition, talent, and possession pales in comparison.

Not even the Bible makes rational sense. We read of characters plagued by doubt, full of violence, making memorable mistakes, interacting with the Divine, and receiving extraordinary glimpses of a supernatural world. We don't get it, and we won't ever get it unless we climb to higher ground. Without this perspective, if we don't understand what His kingdom is about, our spiritual journey is doomed.

Today we are invited to climb the mount of blessing. From there, things look different. We can't go very far on our spiritual journey without the right perspective before understanding the essence of who we are, who God is, and being at peace with where we are and where we ought to be.

Application

How can we be assured that we have the right perspective in life and in our spiritual experience? (Proverbs 23:26; Isaiah 48:18; Romans 12:1, 2)

A prayer for perspective

Lord, I'm confused by the overwhelming amount of information that challenges what I think—even what I've come to believe. Please raise me above this busy valley of human existence and help me connect to You as the true source of spiritual discernment. Let me sit at Your feet and learn from You the principles of Your kingdom. Help me make You my true north, my Guide, and my sure foundation.

A Change in Perspective

What we might include in a prayer for perspective:
- Seeking spiritual clarity
- Learning to recognize God's voice
- Deciding that He must come first in our lives

---

1. James Rowland Angell, "Psychology: Chapter 6: Perception," Mead Project, accessed January 17, 2018, https://brocku.ca/MeadProject/Angell/Angell_1906/Angell_1906_f.html.

The beatitudes were His greeting to the whole human family. Looking upon the vast throng gathered to listen to the Sermon on the Mount, He seemed for the moment to have forgotten that He was not in heaven, and He used the familiar salutation of the world of light. From His lips flowed blessings as the gushing forth of a long-sealed fountain.

—Ellen G. White, *Education*

Chapter 2

The Kingdom Mind

Now when Jesus saw the crowds,
he went up on a mountainside and sat down.
His disciples came to him,
and he began to teach them.
—Matthew 5:1, 2

In June 2017, my wife and I made a trip to the Holy Land. It was a trip we had contemplated for many years but felt apprehensive about undertaking due to the permanent unrest in Israeli-Arab relations. Since the installation of the modern Jewish state in 1948 and the Six-Day War of 1967, the best efforts of diplomats from the United States and Middle Eastern Islamic countries have maintained constrained stability held together with threats, fatwas, and promises of international aid.

Our trip was not lacking in drama. Our first morning in Israel brought the commotion of a murder and suicide in our hotel! Apparently, an older Jewish couple couldn't, or wouldn't, face a future worse than death. When our tour bus took us into Palestinian territories, we couldn't miss the large signs prohibiting the entrance of all Jewish citizens.

The beginning of the Sabbath at the Western Wall was an amazing revelation of the Jewish excitement for their religion, their traditions, and their land. Throngs of young men joined arms as they danced in circles and sang psalms in Hebrew. A long partition separated their revelry from the women, who smiled and prayed and talked in the other half of the huge courtyard.

The next few days were filled with visits to Masada, Jericho, the Sea of Galilee, the Dead Sea, Capernaum, and finally, Jerusalem— the self-proclaimed capital of both Palestine and Israel. Its name means "City of Peace," a name arguably far removed from a description of its historical reality. A couple of days later, a young Israeli policewoman was gunned down at one of the city's ancient gates, and even we tourists, who were carefully guarded against the ugliness of age-old resentments, couldn't help but notice the dozens of heavily armed police encamped inside a wire fence enclosure not more than two hundred yards from the Jaffa Gate.

This incident provoked a reaction from the Jewish religious class, giving our group a dramatic display of Jewish-Islamic animosity. In the long line to enter the Temple Mount and see the famed Dome of the Rock up close, we noticed a group of young Hasidic males cutting in ahead of us. Minutes later, we saw them singing and shouting at the Muslim pilgrims surrounding the golden mosque. Their provocation was so brash that our group was hurriedly rushed out of the grounds through a secondary gate and into streets that didn't look as tourist oriented as some of the others. To us, Jerusalem was wonderful, mystical, beautiful, and challenging. But a "City of Peace" it certainly wasn't.

A clue to the why of the age-old turmoil can perhaps be found in the city's "official" history. To Christians visiting the old city of Jerusalem, especially those paying close attention to the narrative displayed on Israeli-controlled museum placards and by the light shows projected on the ancient stone walls, there is one glaring omission: Jesus is seldom mentioned or acknowledged. It is as if His passage through history was an inconsequential event paling in comparison with the exploits of Jewish military leaders.

The Kingdom Mind

The fact that Christian pilgrims provide the greatest source of revenue to the Israeli tourism industry should suggest otherwise. The life and teachings of Jesus had such a colossal effect on history that, beginning in the fifth century, most historians use Christ's birth (AD, *Anno Domini*, year of our Lord) as the beginning of a new era.

Close to two thousand years ago, within walking distance of the Sea of Galilee, a group more than ten thousand strong crept up the soft hills to fill a valley in expectation of the teachings of a young rabbi from Nazareth with the name Yeshua, a derivative of the fairly common "Joshua." It happened early in Jesus' ministry. It is the first of five discourses in Matthew (the others are found in Matthew 10; 13; 18; and 24). He had called His disciples (chapter 4) and had been preaching with great success throughout Galilee (verse 23). This day He sees that the crowds have grown and are anxious to hear His words. To accommodate them, He climbs to the highest hill, and surrounded by His new inner circle, He raises His voice and speaks.

Our group found our way up the same hills and stopped, partly under the shade of a lonely tree, to remember the words that changed the world—the manifesto of God's kingdom. The Sermon on the Mount is as powerful and subversive today as when it spilled in full strength Aramaic from the lips of Jesus.

The multitude struggling to hear the words of the young Teacher from heaven was as devoid of peace as are today's inhabitants of the Holy Land. Their nation faltered under the heavy burden of Roman occupation and regional politics. A religion loaded with hundreds of self-serving and works-oriented rules had not counteracted the weight of pessimism and despair of people oppressed by the empire.

Jesus saw that they were "like sheep without a shepherd" (Matthew 9:36). Their lives unrolled in the endless monotony of survival, interrupted by the platitudes of religious leaders

21

determined to preserve their own standing.

It's true that religion is a human attempt to bridge the divide between our physical existence and the divine. But true religion must be based on divine content. Its authority must come from revelation. When religion takes human form, it is no longer effective; it just doesn't work. Jesus' listeners needed an injection of divine content into their religious experience.

Ellen White puts it this way: "The beatitudes were His greeting to the whole human family. Looking upon the vast throng gathered to listen to the Sermon on the Mount, He seemed for the moment to have forgotten that He was not in heaven, and He used the familiar salutation of the world of light. From His lips flowed blessings as the gushing forth of a long-sealed fountain."[1]

Although the Beatitudes are a divine recipe for human happiness, that's not their intent. The "pursuit of happiness" ensconced in the United States' Declaration of Independence was not contemplated in the reality of first-century life. In fact, when men and women sat among the low shrubbery of the Galilean landscape, the "happiness" they were seeking was a political solution to Roman control and heavy taxation.

Jesus would disappoint them.

We, too, would be disappointed by the meaning of Jesus' words. In essence, their promise of God's favor to the downtrodden, the humbled, the oppressed, and the bullied reads like the worst recipe for success in our dog-eat-dog Western culture.

Here are Jesus' words, as they appear in Matthew 5:2–10, interspersed with my attempts at possible counterinterpretations that better describe the sentiment of our times:

"Blessed are the poor in spirit, for theirs is the kingdom of heaven."
Be strong, and you will take this world by storm.

"Blessed are those who mourn, for they will be comforted."
Don't let anybody see you sweat; you can deal with your own feelings.

"Blessed are the meek, for they will inherit the earth."
Be confident and go big, and you will build a fortune.

"Blessed are those who hunger and thirst for righteousness, for they will be filled."
Accept that life isn't fair and human nature is what it is.

"Blessed are the merciful, for they will be shown mercy."
You have a purpose. If somebody gets in your way, too bad for them.

"Blessed are the pure in heart, for they will see God."
As long as you aren't hurting anyone, it's fine. Morality is just a construct.

"Blessed are the peacemakers, for they will be called children of God."
If they hit you, hit them back twice as hard.

"Blessed are those who are persecuted because of righteousness, for theirs is the kingdom of heaven."
Do your thing; just don't get in trouble.

Do you see how this advice may have deflated the patriotic desires of His audience? Could anyone build an earthly government on such a celebration of the human predicament? Can you imagine a modern politician dedicating attention to these ideals, giving such hope to the poorest, the saddest, and perhaps the most insignificant members of society? This is no way to build a kingdom . . . at least, not an earthly one.

The Sermon on the Mount seems to speak of happiness, but we soon realize that it is not the human definition of happiness. It teaches us that the key to human well-being is based not on circumstances or things but in being an object of God's blessings.

The word *blessed* means to have God's approval. The contentment we seek comes from being right with God. This is true well-being. It is based on a right relationship with God. This "blessedness" is what allows certain individuals to go through the most horrible circumstances and still maintain peace, quiet, and confidence in the midst of anything and everything.

The message of the Sermon on the Mount, starting with the Beatitudes, has a timeless quality. It still speaks to us in the midst of our worries and disappointments. It doesn't ignore the fact that we need material things. In the language of psychology, we need food, shelter, affection, belonging. The heavenly Father knows that we need all these things, but we ought not to seek them first. We must first seek the kingdom of God and His righteousness. As a consequence, we will receive all these things (Matthew 6:28–33).

Jesus wants to adjust our perspective. We can't grow in spirit and righteousness when we don't understand the basics. We are seeking a heavenly kingdom with different rules. True happiness cannot be based on circumstance. Here is how Ellen White puts it: "Happiness drawn from earthly sources is as changeable as varying circumstances can make it; but the peace of Christ is a constant and abiding peace. It does not depend upon any circumstances in life, on the amount of worldly goods or the number of earthly friends. Christ is the fountain of living water, and happiness drawn from Him can never fail."[2]

In the next chapters, we will explore a spiritual path that will take us to a progressive understanding of our spiritual needs and encourage in us an attitude conducive to spiritual growth and renewed purpose. Following is a representation of the kingdom journey that awaits us in the study of the blessings of Matthew 5.

The kingdom journey

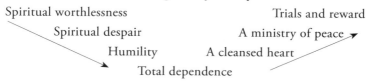

Spiritual worthlessness   Trials and reward

     Spiritual despair   A ministry of peace

       Humility   A cleansed heart

         Total dependence

Application

1. What kind of happiness are the Beatitudes promising? (Matthew 6:33; John 16:33)

2. Is blessedness something we can achieve or the result of a relationship with the One who blesses us? (John 15:4, 5)

A prayer for understanding God's kingdom

Lord, create in me a kingdom mind. Please let me hear Your voice among and above any other, calling me to submission and trust. Let me realize that my deepest interests are not aligned with this world. Yes, I yearn for change and justice and a better life for me and others, but help me understand that I'm just passing through. As beautiful as this world may be, nothing can compare with living in the blessedness of Your presence.

What we might include in a prayer for understanding God's kingdom

- Seeking to know when my interests are in conflict with God's plan
- Learning to distinguish between the transitory and the eternal
- Developing a sense of gratitude for blessings of the spirit or material blessings

---

1. Ellen G. White, *Education* (Oakland, CA: Pacific Press®, 1903), 79.
2. Ellen G. White, *Thoughts From the Mount of Blessing*, 16.

Jesus' words in the Sermon on the Mount

challenge humanity's core values. Instead of

self-reliance, they speak of relying on God;

instead of human ingenuity, they propose

divine providence. God's blessings are given

to those who desperately need them.

—p. 30

Chapter 3

The Pain of Unworthiness

"Blessed are the poor in spirit,
for theirs is the kingdom of heaven."
—Matthew 5:3

Christians have always been accused of being weak. Karl Marx said Christianity was the "opium of the masses." The idea is that it's something we made up to cope, that we need belief to function. It's meant as criticism, but is it unfounded?

In 1978 Pastor John Piper spoke to a group of Inter-Varsity students and people off the street in Aspen, Colorado. At the conclusion of his talk, one of his students asked a common question: "Isn't Christianity a crutch for people who can't make it on their own?" Pastor Piper smiled and said: "Yes." Period[1].[1]

What's wrong with a crutch? I had a pair of crutches behind my office door for years after having foot surgery sometime in the nineties. As I remember it, the crutches were wonderful! Crutches are fine when you are a cripple and have a hard time standing without them.

The problem is that needing a crutch goes with a condition of powerlessness. It entails a certain deficiency that makes assistance indispensable. But when used correctly, crutches allow a level of movement not available without them.

The idea that the Christian faith is a crutch for the weak or the opium of the masses presumes that the intended goal for human beings is self-reliance, self-confidence, and self-determination—all of which lead to self-esteem.[2] This idea presumes that to feel valued and fulfilled, one ought to seek strength, independence, and the admiration of others.

Jesus' words in the Sermon on the Mount challenge humanity's core values. Instead of self-reliance, they speak of relying on God; instead of human ingenuity, they propose divine providence. God's blessings are given to those who desperately need them. Thus, being "poor in spirit" is absolutely crucial to our spiritual journey.

What is being poor? By definition, poverty refers to the lack of things, necessary things. There is perceived poverty, and there is absolute poverty. In dollars and cents, the United States government places the 2020 poverty level at $12,760 per one person and $26,200 for a family of four.[2] It is deemed that a person or persons whose income falls below these figures would have difficulties covering basic necessities like food, utilities, and accommodation. In comparison, in a country like Cuba, where the unofficial per capita income is around $360 per year, a family with a yearly income of $26,000 would be markedly well off.

For many in an affluent society, being "poor" is usually a feeling tied to one's inability to afford nice, quality "stuff" or the latest technology. Poverty is relative. One thing I learned from one of my earliest university courses in sociology was that poverty is more than an income level; it is also a culture. Being poor generally correlates with certain attitudes about education, a feeling of hopelessness, and living in survival mode.

But not always. It is possible to have a poverty-level income and not be culturally poor. Many life-enriching experiences are not costly: reading, exercising, or spending time with loved ones. What this tells us is that being poor is more than a number. It is also a perception or an acknowledgment.

The Pain of Unworthiness

Being poor in spirit is a perception of need. But it is not entirely relative. Spiritual poverty is "absolute" poverty. This is how Ellen White refers to it:

> The poor in spirit are those who claim no personal merit, and boast of no virtue in themselves. Realizing their utter helplessness, and deeply convicted of sin, they put no faith in mere outward ceremonies, but cast themselves upon Jesus who is all-righteous and all-compassionate. The Christian can only rise through humility. The proud heart strives in vain to earn salvation by good works; for though one cannot be saved without good works, yet these alone will not suffice to win eternal life. After he has done all he can, Christ must impute to him his own righteousness.[3]

Spiritual poverty is an acknowledgment of "utter helplessness," the recognition of having "no personal merit," and a deep conviction of sin. The recognition of spiritual poverty is a prerequisite of salvation. Jesus said, "It is not the healthy who need a doctor, but the sick. I have not come to call the righteous, but sinners" (Mark 2:17). The description of His overarching purpose was "to seek and to save the lost" (Luke 19:10).

There are at least three facets of spiritual poverty: a lack of spiritual standing, the condition of spiritual emptiness, and the inability to become spiritually rich by ourselves.

Could it be that a wrong understanding of salvation neutralizes the efficacy of our spiritual walk? Is it possible that believing we can contribute to the salvation process somehow makes it harder for God to bless us?

Let's look at a classic passage:

> "Two men went up to the temple to pray, one a Pharisee and the other a tax collector. The Pharisee stood by himself

31

and prayed: 'God, I thank you that I am not like other people—robbers, evildoers, adulterers—or even like this tax collector. I fast twice a week and give a tenth of all I get.'

"But the tax collector stood at a distance. He would not even look up to heaven, but beat his breast and said, 'God, have mercy on me, a sinner.'

"I tell you that this man, rather than the other, went home justified before God. For all those who exalt themselves will be humbled, and those who humble themselves will be exalted" (Luke 18:10–14).

All around us, the ethos of self-reliance, the concept of standing up for ourselves, of realizing our full potential, stands in contrast with the message of the Beatitudes. This human need to be self-sufficient, to make it, to be in charge of our destiny, does not serve us well in the spiritual realm.

The first step toward a blessed spiritual life is acknowledging our "utter helplessness," being able to meaningfully say: "Lord, have mercy on me, for I am a sinner."

Bible saints struck this chord again and again. When Abraham pleaded with God to save Sodom and Gomorrah, he said: "I have been so bold as to speak to the Lord, though I am nothing but dust and ashes" (Genesis 18:27). As Jacob prepared to meet Esau and his four hundred men, he prayed: "I am unworthy of all the kindness and faithfulness you have shown your servant" (Genesis 32:10). When called to serve God as His prophet through a vision in the temple, Isaiah answered: "Woe to me! . . . . I am ruined! For I am a man of unclean lips, and I live among a people of unclean lips, and my eyes have seen the King, the LORD Almighty" (Isaiah 6:5).

In a prayer of repentance and deep understanding of his lack of standing before the Lord, David wrote:

Have mercy on me, O God,
    according to your unfailing love;
according to your great compassion
    blot out my transgressions.
Wash away all my iniquity
    and cleanse me from my sin.

For I know my transgressions,
    and my sin is always before me (Psalm 51:1–3).

Is this inadequacy only temporary? Does this prayer apply only to the recognition of great sins? Is there a moment when we have been forgiven and are no longer "poor in spirit"? The better question would be: Do we ever reach a point when we need the Lord any less?

The message from the mount of blessing starts here, with the need to understand our basic dependence on God. God cannot fill a vessel that's already full. The heart that will be blessed will not interpose its own importance or claim its ability to obey. The steps in the ladder to spiritual success and powerful prayer are headed downward before heading up.

Ellen White wrote:

Jesus had presented the cup of blessing to those who felt that they were "rich, and increased with goods" (Revelation 3:17), and had need of nothing, and they had turned with scorn from the gracious gift. He who feels whole, who thinks that he is reasonably good, and is contented with his condition, does not seek to become a partaker of the grace and righteousness of Christ. Pride feels no need, and so it closes the heart against Christ and the infinite blessings He came to give. There is no room for Jesus in the heart of such a person. Those who are rich and honorable in their own eyes do not ask in faith, and receive the blessing of God. They feel that they are full, therefore they go away empty.[4]

You and I are poor in spirit. The only thing we bring to the salvation equation is our own wretched selves—full of pride, perpetually self-centered, manipulative, conniving, empty. Here, repeat with me: "I am lacking. I am spiritually bankrupt, I am morally unclean, I am unworthy before God." Difficult, isn't it? The answer to spiritual poverty is not better self-esteem. Jesus doesn't offer platitudes to calm our sense of worthlessness. He doesn't tell us, "You are good; you are somebody; you can do it!" Instead, He says, "My grace is sufficient for you, for my power is made perfect in weakness" (2 Corinthians 12:9).

Rather than tell us that the answer is within us, He says:

"Do not fear, for I am with you;
    do not be dismayed, for I am your God.
I will strengthen you and help you;
    I will uphold you with my righteous right hand" (Isaiah
    41:10).

It's that simple. It's all about Him. He is rich; we are poor. He is the "Father of the heavenly lights," from whom flow all "good and perfect" gifts (James 1:17); we are like the Canaanite woman who aspired only to the crumbs falling from the master's table (Matthew 15:21–28).

The Messiah's words were a threat to religious self-righteousness. In His audience, some were immune to the heavenly blessings flowing from His lips, while others realized that this message was like water to their thirsty souls, that true joy and fulfillment come only from God and His grace. Then and now, everyone is "poor in spirit," but only those who realize it will be blessed.

Application

1. Should I feel ashamed of my deep need of God? (Romans 1:16, 17)

2. Is the ultimate purpose of acknowledging our helplessness to make us feel miserable? What about the promise to the poor in spirit? (Matthew 5:3)

A prayer of desperation

Lord, it's hard to admit that I'm lacking. Being poor in spirit goes beyond the rejection of pride; it means sinking much lower, to a place of prostration and bewilderment. I can be proud of many things, but spiritual wealth is not one of them. Although I'm richly blessed by the certainty of Your Spirit all around me, I'm also always lacking, always needy, ever fighting the reality of my weakness and my selfish nature. Please keep me focused on the fact that where I'm weak, You are exceedingly strong.

What we might include in a prayer of desperation

- Learning to admit our true condition
- Expressing our need for God's mercy
- Rejecting our spiritual pride

---

1. John Piper, "Blessed Are the Poor in Spirit Who Mourn," Desiring God, February 2, 1986, https://www.desiringgod.org/messages/blessed-are-the-poor -in-spirit-who-mourn.

2. Piper.

3. "Federal Poverty Level (FPL)," HealthCare.gov, accessed January 17, 2021, https://www.healthcare.gov/glossary/federal-poverty-level-FPL/.

4. Ellen G. White, *The Spirit of Prophecy*, vol. 2 (Battle Creek, MI: Seventh-day Adventist Publishing Association, 1877), 204, 205.

5. Ellen G. White, *Thoughts From the Mount of Blessing*, 7.

At Mount Horeb and Sinai, God came down,

and a few chosen people were allowed to

climb up to Him on holy mountains revered for

centuries, amid thunder and lightning. Here,

God climbs up to a common mountain by

the Sea of Galilee, and people are allowed

near Him, almost touching Him, because He

is already there with His people. He speaks

loudly because there are many, but His voice

is peaceful and still and soothing to the heart.

—p. 39

Chapter 4

Sad for the Right Reasons

"Blessed are those who mourn,
for they will be comforted."
—Matthew 5:4

In the early spring of 1992, I experienced my first real taste of full-strength grieving. My wife and I were walking with our small children through a soccer field when a call came to my cell phone from my mother in South Florida. Her words were sudden, abrupt, and full of hopelessness: "Your grandfather died."

I don't know exactly which chemical substances are dumped into our bloodstream by our glands at such a moment, but the pain was so raw and physical that I dropped to the ground in front of my family as if punched in the stomach. My grandparents raised me after my parents' divorce, and my grandfather had been the most stable and solid human presence in my life during my childhood and teenage years. A man of few words and enviable honesty and work ethics, he and his brothers had built a bus company that ferried passengers across the length of the island nation of Cuba.

I've grieved over other relatives since then, and as a pastor, I've conducted many funerals before and after. Still, that first close encounter with death's profound impact was unlike anything I had ever experienced. How can Jesus say that those who mourn are blessed? How can we equate the deepest sadness with spiritual well-being?

The New Testament uses nine different words to convey the idea of *sadness*. The word used in Matthew 5:4 refers to the deepest kind of sadness, the cry of a broken heart. This is the sadness we avoid, the sadness we don't know how to deal with in others, the utter despair that drains our psychological resources and leaves us unable to move.

In His sermon, Jesus is proposing a revolutionary concept: that sadness is not incompatible with joy. A world without God can equate happiness only with good feelings; we are either happy or wretched, laughing or crying, enjoying well-being or in misery, prancing at the top of the mountain or hanging on for dear life to avoid falling into the abyss.

People are seen as being in one of two camps: the fortunate and the unfortunate. Life is a game we play with the hand we were given. Happiness is mostly a product of good genes, a strong family, the right circumstances, being at the right place at the right time. It is externally driven. We are basically happy when things go well often enough, when we have learned to reasonably expect good outcomes.

We form the opinion that the blessed must be the rich and famous, the ones with the constant smile, the triumphant, the ones who are honored by the world. We covet their luck, we follow their journey, we come to accept their superior fate. Sometimes we pine for their success because we feel that at least some of us ought to be that fortunate.

But here is Jesus, who has been going from village to village healing people, speaking with grace and power. He climbs a mountain and invites the crowd to come closer so that He can share with them something different. He comes to correct a fundamental error. He is proposing a new paradigm whereby blessedness is not equated with good fortune. The gospel can bring happiness to every heart, even the ones assaulted by grief and sadness.

Jesus is making everything new (Revelation 21:5). He is doing things differently. Instead of pronouncing His blessings at the end of the sermon to dismiss the people, Jesus blesses them at the beginning to attract them. What He is going to say is going to change things. From their history, they had learned the cost of disobedience, that it was far better to obey (see Deuteronomy 27; 28). Now they will understand why. The black and white of the Old Testament will yield to the full-color realism of the true kingdom of God—a spiritual place of deeper meaning and connection, of better explanations and stronger hope.

At Mount Horeb and Sinai, God came down, and a few chosen people were allowed to climb up to Him on these holy mountains revered for centuries, amid thunder and lightning. Here, *God* climbs up to a common mountain by the Sea of Galilee, and people are allowed near Him, almost touching Him, because He is already there with His people. He speaks loudly because there are many, but His voice is peaceful and still and soothing to the heart.

He is no ordinary high priest who ministers before God to open the channels of His blessings; He has the power to bless. When He pronounces a blessing on us, we are blessed indeed. The power of thunder and lightning has been distilled into words of life as consequential and earth-shaking as Creation itself.

But the spiritual nature of His message requires a spiritual interpretation of our sadness. Just as happiness is not based on circumstances or external conditions, the mourning that elicits God's comforting is not always circumstantial. There is sadness that may not be comforted, which falls outside of God's intent in His promise. Paul tells us that there are two kinds of sadness. "Godly sorrow brings repentance that leads to salvation and leaves no regret, but worldly sorrow brings death" (2 Corinthians 7:10).

It may be normal or acceptable to despair for frivolous or superficial reasons, but we shouldn't expect to be comforted by God when our sadness arises from these. God will not bless you in any significant way if your favorite team lost the Super Bowl or your hair coloring didn't come out just right or you hit your finger with a hammer.

We may be sad when we are denied something we crave—a new promotion that never transpired, a failed offer on the house we really wanted, a lower grade than we think we deserved, the weight that doesn't come off.

Sometimes our wishes can be so carnal that asking for God's blessing may be an aberration. Amnon was so obsessed with a forbidden lust for his half-sister Tamar that he became physically ill (2 Samuel 13:2). Ahab was saddened to the point that he refused to eat because he couldn't possess Naboth's land (1 Kings 21:4).

There is the sadness of false repentance when we regret the consequences rather than the wrongness of sin. We become sad when caught in the act or when facing the punishment of our actions. Here is the adulterer who misses time with his children, the abuser who feels the weight of a restraining order, the petty thief confronted by the store's security guard and the shame of spending time in prison.

Godly sorrow is the pain of feeling separated from God, of knowing ourselves sinners in dire need of grace and forgiveness. Isaiah 59 offers one of the sharpest descriptions of the sin state in the Scriptures:

So justice is far from us,
    and righteousness does not reach us.
We look for light, but all is darkness;

for brightness, but we walk in deep shadows.
Like the blind we grope along the wall,
 feeling our way like people without eyes.
At midday we stumble as if it were twilight;
 among the strong, we are like the dead.
We all growl like bears;
 we moan mournfully like doves.
We look for justice, but find none;
 for deliverance, but it is far away.

For our offenses are many in your sight,
 and our sins testify against us.
Our offenses are ever with us,
 and we acknowledge our iniquities (verses 9–12).

We should mourn over this. We cannot be at rest when we wander from God. It pains us, and it pains Him. There is no peace without repentance; blessedness is incompatible with sin.

The sanctuary service showed us that before bringing any offering into God's presence, the priests had to wash their hands at the bronze basin. "He [Moses] placed the basin between the tent of meeting and the altar and put water in it for washing, and Moses and Aaron and his sons used it to wash their hands and feet. They washed whenever they entered the tent of meeting or approached the altar, as the Lord commanded Moses" (Exodus 40:30–32). The washing of hands and feet may not have been as prominent in the sanctuary service as other instructions in Leviticus, but it needed to happen first.

Before we minister, we must be washed. A meaningful spiritual life must start with the washing of our sins in the crimson fountain of the blood of the Lamb. To come fully into God's holy place, we must first visit the basin and carry before us the incense of our heartfelt prayers. He pleads with us:

"Come now, let us settle the matter." . . .
"Though your sins are like scarlet,
  they shall be as white as snow;
though they are red as crimson,
  they shall be like wool" (Isaiah 1:18).

Godly sorrow is the sorrow that God Himself shares. This is when we feel moved by human pain, shaken by tribulations and trials, hurt by evil's oppression. I remember listening to a presentation by Pat Arrabito at an ASI convention a few years ago. Pat and her husband founded a video ministry that has produced arguably the best documentary on the history of the seventh-day Sabbath.* In an unassuming tone of voice, a self-professed introvert, Pat told the story of a tragedy that shook her life to the core.

In August 1990, her husband, James, and their two sons, thirteen-year-old Tony and eleven-year-old Joey, flew from Los Angeles to Anchorage, Alaska. James was working on a documentary and wanted to obtain some footage.

When they didn't arrive on Monday, Pat and her brother started calling the authorities in Anchorage. No one knew what had happened, except that the six-passenger Cessna had not landed at the airport. The night before, on Sunday, a storm had crushed Anchorage. The pilot called the airport for help, but the plane was blown off course and minutes later crashed into the rocky side of the Talkeetna mountains.

Pat and her two other children waited anxiously at their home in Northern California. Sometime in the afternoon, her brother found out that the plane had been sighted and that a sheriff in California had been contacted to come to the Arrabito's home

---

* LLT Productions, founded by James Arrabito, completed in 2005 *The Seventh Day: Revelations From the Lost Pages of History*, a five-part documentary series tracing the story of the Bible Sabbath.

to share the information. Upon the insistence of Pat's brother, the sheriff allowed him to bear the news to the family.

In an interview with Dwight Nelson, Pat describes the moment when her brother and father arrived at the house where other family members had gathered:

My brother just said there were no survivors. And I just heard those words just whirling around in my head over and over. You know? "No survivors, no survivors, no survivors." And then I'm thinking: *Yes, there are survivors because there are me and my other two children.* And I don't know how long we were out there. It was kind of a timeless time.

I went back in the house, and my kids had been sitting on people's laps. They came over. My daughter was almost nine; my son, seven. And they just both came over and climbed on my lap, and I hugged them, and my son said, "My daddy's dead, isn't he?" And I just nodded, and my daughter said, "And Tony and Joey?"

I said, "Yeah." You know, there was just such a huge sense of "How can this be true? How can somebody who was just there . . . not be anymore?"

You know, it's almost like you're in another world. I can't even describe the sense of floating in space and time. . . . It was just overwhelming. It was really hard to go to bed that night. It was really hard to go to bed and know that I was going to go to bed alone from then on. It was hard for my kids to sleep. They both climbed into bed with me. In fact, they climbed in bed with me for the next year. They didn't want to sleep alone.

I can't describe the feelings that I had trying to go to sleep. I think it took me quite a while. But in the midst of it all, there was still a sense that God was right there. I had such a sense of God's presence. And it was an odd thing to me. I mean, it was noteworthy that in the midst of the most agonizing experience I think I could ever have, I still felt this center of peace within me and a sense that God was right there. And that whatever agony I was enduring, God was too. He was right there with me, enduring it. And I wasn't alone.

There are lots of things I can't answer about God, but I know that He's good, and I know that He has been there. You know, He carried me. And I told Him, "You have to just keep carrying me because I cannot walk alone." And He's carried me ever since.[1]

Speaking at ASI, Pat said that when she and her small children embraced in the middle of the room, it felt as if the pain of the whole world had concentrated in their little group hug. I trust and pray that God is still carrying Pat and her children, now adults, in His arms.

We are not naïve. Pain and sorrow and sadness are all around us, and many times *in* us. There is no life without pain. Love is pain. Beauty is pain. Healing is pain. We are struggling and striving. There is none among us who hasn't eaten their bread mixed with tears (Psalm 102:9) or spent a moonless night in weeping prayer. But Jesus promised that those who mourn will be comforted. This sadness is not our final state, and not even death is the final act. It can't be. John the revelator says it clearly:

Then I saw "a new heaven and a new earth," for the first heaven and the first earth had passed away, and there was no longer any sea. I saw the Holy City, the new Jerusalem, coming down out of heaven from God, prepared as a bride beautifully dressed for her husband. And I heard a loud voice from the throne saying, "Look! God's dwelling place is now among the people, and he will dwell with them. They will be his people, and God himself will be with them and be their God. '*He will wipe every tear from their eyes. There will be no more death' or mourning or crying or pain,* for the old order of things has passed away" (Revelation 21:1–4; emphasis added).

Application
Can we expect to be comforted in our sadness in the here and now? (Matthew 11:28, 29)

A prayer of pain and sorrow
My God, why do I sometimes feel so utterly abandoned? Why am I blinded by pain so deep that I can't feel Your presence? Even though I understand that I'm not to be free from tribulation in this life, how come it hurts so much when I'm traversing it? I'm not asking that You make me insensitive to sorrow; all I ask is that I'm able to discern Your holy presence in my fiery furnace. I want You here as a Friend, as the Rock I can lean on when my strength is gone. And I know that comfort is coming.

What we might include in a prayer for pain and sorrow
- Realizing that blessedness is not synonymous with well-being or good feelings
- Allowing God to carry us when we can't carry on
- Expressing the hope of ultimate joy in God's presence

---

1. Pat Arrabito and Dwight Nelson, "On God and Dying," *The Evidence*, Faith for Today, 2001 http://www.faithfortoday.tv/article/63/programs/archives/the-evidence/episodes/episode-108-god-and-dying/guest-information/episode-108-god-and-dying-v2. (Web page discontinued.)

Jesus modeled what constitutes a meek spirit.

Meekness is not a natural tendency to quiet

passivity. It is not complacency before a

violation of principle. It is being calm in the

face of life's challenges; it is being submissive

to the Spirit, being forgiving and patient in

seeking to do God's will.

—p. 51

Chapter 5

The Prayer of Humility

"Blessed are the meek,
for they will inherit the earth."
—Matthew 5:5

Like other ministerial interns, I struggled to implement theory in a real-life church setting in my first years of ministry. I served as a Bible worker for over a year and was then placed as a youth pastor in a metropolitan church of considerable size. One important part of our training was learning to support the ministries carried out from the conference office and learning from the various leadership styles displayed by our elders. One particular conference leader left a considerable impression on my young heart. Short of stature and somewhat portly, he spoke loudly and often made fun of the aspiring ministers. Charismatic and critical, eloquent and dismissive—more than once, I fell victim to his wit and sarcasm.

He should have known that Adventism is a movement. A conference session came, and the delegates decided to make significant changes in leadership. Most top-level leaders were replaced, and the sharp-tongued wonder was left in limbo. To this day, I feel fortunate that I didn't gloat at his loss of influence. God's ways are a mystery, and several months later, in his new role as itinerant pastoral staff, this man temporarily became my assistant in my brand new district! At twenty-three years of age, I learned never to make fun of anyone younger or less experienced than myself.

Decades later, our society still doesn't do meekness well. We all want a gold medal; silver and bronze winners serve only to showcase the person at the top during the awards ceremony. We instill a competitive instinct in our children from the moment they enter into group relationships. They are graded, measured, evaluated, and compared to each other in academics, sports, and demeanor. True, we want to help our children develop into productive human beings, but these requirements to measure up to a standard begin to define our sense of worth. Later, as adults, sometimes we are consumed by the need for recognition, or a place at the top or, at the very minimum, the admiration of others. Our well-being and even our identity become attached to our achievements or status.

Our age of social media has created a world of protagonists. Every Twitter, Facebook, or Instagram account is a statement of personhood, a telling of one's life in the tenuous pages of the worldwide web. Every "like," comment, or endorsement is an instant evaluation of our lives. We are affirmed by our number of followers, our internet footprint. In 2013, there were 152 million blogs on the web. In January 2018, there were 392 million.* This enormous mass of opinionated content exacerbates the difficulty of finding a true voice of reason or inspiration. We have eaten the forbidden fruit and have become little gods unto ourselves (Genesis 3:5).

The third beatitude, like the others, is as much a promise as

---

* Blogging.org and statista.com listed the number of blogs as roughly 300 million in 2020. The total number of websites and blogs fluctuate around 1.5 billion (close to one per every six persons living on the planet). "Total Number of Websites," Internet Live Stats, http://www.internetlivestats.com/total-number -of-websites.

a statement of fact. Meekness is both a condition of inheritance and a quality of God's heirs to the kingdom. The meek will inherit the earth because being with God is all they really want. What matters is His will, not theirs.

On February 7, 2005, the funeral of Pastor Manuel Vásquez, a long-time Seventh-day Adventist Church leader, was held at the General Conference chapel in Silver Spring, Maryland. At the time of his death, Pastor Vásquez served as a vice president of the North American Division, with oversight of Multilingual Ministries. He presided over a period of accelerated growth in the number of ethnic churches and foreign-born members of the denomination. He was an avid reader. He wrote several books on the dangers of the New Age and a comprehensive history of the church's mission among Hispanics in the United States and Canada.[1]

For almost ten years, Elder Vásquez had been battling cancer. After aggressive treatments at the Loma Linda Medical Center, he enjoyed several years of ministry aided by a healthy lifestyle and daily jogging. Bob Kyte, president of Pacific Press at the time, asked me to represent the publishing house at his memorial service, where many who had known Elder Vásquez over many years took some time to honor their friend and his life of service.

Perhaps the most emotional moment of the program was when his wife, Nancy, his companion for four decades, told of a conversation he had with his doctor. The physician, who was now the bearer of the worst possible news, finally confronted him, saying, "Pastor Vásquez, I know that you and your family are praying for a miracle. But what if a miracle does not happen?" Pastor Vásquez replied, "My faith will remain the same." He knew God and knew he could trust Him.

This is meekness. To be meek is to accept the will of God for us without disputing or resisting. To be meek is to acknowledge that what happens to us has been permitted by God and that

He will use it for His honor and glory. We need to know and accept God's sovereignty. Being meek means allowing God to be in control of every detail of our life: our marriage, our children, our work, our health, our spiritual life. To be meek is to say, "Not my will be done, but Yours."

The promise to the meek contains several layers of meaning. For one, it could be a statement of psychological fact. Maybe it's telling us that it is actually healthier to be unassuming, gentle, and humble. Maybe being less affected by the need to defend our worth and impose our will is in itself a recipe for winning at the game of life.

Let's also clarify that being meek is not synonymous with being spineless. The greatest paragons of meekness in Scripture were far from yellow bellies. Moses, the meekest man (Numbers 12:3), was a strong, vigorous leader who faced forty years of exile, a perilous confrontation with the mighty Pharaoh, and forty years of wandering in the wilderness, facing constant rebellion and ungratefulness.

Jesus declared Himself to be meek (Matthew 11:29), and some Middle Age artists represented Him as a pale, pasty, sad figure. Nothing could be further from the truth; Jesus was no weakling in any sense of the word. The Greek word *praus,* translated in verse 29 as "gentle" (NIV), means controlled strength. For Christ, it meant submission to a degree mere humans could never comprehend. For a Being whose very nature was both human and divine, in whom resided the infinite powers of true deity, to hold back the expression of such might during His earthly journey and submit in all things to the Father is one of the great mysteries of the Incarnation.*

He was humble in not employing His power for His own benefit, in not performing miracles when prompted or to satisfy the curiosity of His tormentors, in not acting on His own, and in speaking only the words of the Father (John 8:28).

Jesus modeled what constitutes a meek spirit. Meekness is not a natural tendency to quiet passivity. It is not complacency before a violation of principle. It is being calm in the face of life's challenges; it is being submissive to the Spirit, being forgiving and patient in seeking to do God's will.

The first two beatitudes celebrate the acknowledgment of a deep need of God. Without Him, we are nothing. Meekness follows being poor in spirit and mourning for our sins; in a sense, it is the result of acknowledging our weakness and dependence on God's grace. We are sinners; He is the High Priest who can solve our sin problem. We are helpless; He is the great Helper. We are sick; He is the Great Physician. We are anxious and angry; He is the Prince of Peace.

One of the greatest prayer promises of Scripture is found in 1 John 5:14, 15: "This is the confidence we have in approaching God: that if we ask anything according to his will, he hears us.

---

* Philippians 2:5–8 describes the extraordinary humbling of the second person of the Trinity:

In your relationships with one another, have the same mindset as Christ Jesus:

Who, being in very nature God,
   did not consider equality with God something to be used to his own
      advantage;

rather, he made himself nothing
   by taking the very nature of a servant,
   being made in human likeness.

And being found in appearance as a man,
he humbled himself
by becoming obedient to death—
   even death on a cross!

51

And if we know that he hears us—whatever we ask—we know that we have what we asked of him."

Meekness is what places us in a position where we pray according to God's will; it leads us to conform ourselves to the mind of God and not rebel against the instructions of His Word. Such a humble state is an absolute condition for answered prayers.

We live in a puffed-up world. Pride shows itself in every area of life. We want to take credit for what we perceive as rightfully ours. We cling to positions and possessions. We go through life like puffed-up kernels of cereal, only to be eaten by the unforgiving pain and cruelty of human existence. We are like the grass in the field, mowed down at the end of the season for animal fodder.

The only competition that really matters—the spiritual journey—is not against others. Growth happens inwardly in the indwelling gifts of grace, wisdom, love, and virtue. Meekness toward God manifests itself in meekness toward others. Like the Ten Commandments, it speaks of a vertical connection with God and a horizontal connection to others.

Meekness allows us to follow human leaders. In a "me" society, *authority* is not a nice word. Even in the context of the Christian mission, power struggles are nothing if not common. We speak of "first leaders" (referring in our Adventist lingo to conference, union, and division presidents)—those who serve at the pleasure of their constituents but are allowed to have the last word, or the most influential one, in discussions. Second leaders tend to be seen as symbolic, more involved in bureaucracy, following orders, implementing plans.

Not all second leaders are comfortable in such a position. Most see second-level leadership as a temporary step toward greater power. And people who lose leadership positions sometimes see their "decrease" as a terrible indication of loss of confidence, diminished influence, and prestige. Thus, those who are consumed or concerned with climbing the leadership ladder sometimes fail to enjoy the quiet fruits of humble service, of the anonymous acts of kindness that enrich our lives.

According to God, being meek is acknowledging that roles of lesser prominence do not make us any less special in God's eyes. In His eyes, we are all equal; all have exactly the same intrinsic value. We can be meek because in Him we are strong. In Him, we can do all things (Philippians 4:13). We can also be kind and considerate to those under our care or leadership because we know that they are just as valuable as we are.

Maybe meekness is part of what makes a child more susceptible to the call of God's kingdom. A child's psyche, unencumbered by the adult's complex need to defend their ego, is more able to learn at the feet of Jesus. Notice that the reward of the meek is the same reward promised to children: "Let the little children come to me, and do not hinder them, for the kingdom of heaven belongs to such as these" (Matthew 19:14).

Psychologists and educators talk about "teachable" moments, those occasions when life demands answers and hearts are desperate for comfort. Children are permanently teachable. Their humility, trust, and spontaneity are open channels to the Spirit's promptings. We are to be like children. When we pray, our defenses ought to fall to the hallowed ground of the cross. Then we can receive, our hands unclenched, open to accept His favor. We should pray as children, who look to their parents for everything, unashamedly, undeserving, admiring in wonder the gifts from the Father's heart. Only the children can inherit all things; only they are the rightful heirs. They are the meek; they "will inherit the land and enjoy peace and prosperity" (Psalm 37:11).

Application

Is being meek equivalent to having a low self-esteem? Or is it being able to value ourselves in the light of the cross? (Philippians 3:8)

A prayer of humility

How wonderful it is when my will aligns with Yours, when my heart is beating in cadence with Your great heart. Unfortunately, there are times when this isn't so. In my quest for self-determination, for recognition, for feeling that I am right, I'm often at odds with You. Please let me know when I need to let go and let You take over. It is so comforting, so liberating, to know that life is not about me but about You.

What we might include in a prayer for humility
- Asking for help in letting down our defenses when this is required
- Acknowledging that leadership shouldn't be a goal but a response to a call to service
- Surrendering to God every facet of our lives

---

1. See *The Danger Within* and *The Mainstreaming of the New Age*, available at AdventistBookCenter.com, and *The Untold Story: 100 Years of Hispanic Adventism 1899–1999* (Boise, ID: Pacific Press®, 2000).

Our human spirit can flourish only as a result of accepting our spiritual poverty. We become aware of our perpetual loss, the pain arising from the sin that separates us from our Creator. And we begin to grasp that the way of salvation is of heavenly construction, that our efforts are nothing compared to the rescue operation effected at Calvary and supported by Christ's activity in heaven's sanctuary.

—p. 58

Chapter 6

Thirst for God

"Blessed are those who hunger and thirst for righteousness,
for they will be filled."

—Matthew 5:6

My wife and I have taken lots of selfies as a couple. We often speak of the need to catalog these and label them with their time and place. We have selfies from many places in the United States and a few countries in Europe and the Americas. In some of them, the background is truly spectacular. Both of us look pretty much the same in all the pictures, but the view of the landscape or historical structure behind us is a totally different thing. We enjoy looking at these pictures and remembering the occasion. But as the years go by, these recollections are beginning to lose their clarity, and details become fuzzier.

Just as a picture cannot substitute for the experience of the moment and the emotions associated with what was happening when it was taken, so, spiritually, there is no substitute for the encounter with the reality of God that we crave deep inside ourselves. We know that there is more to life than our own resources and our limited experiences. When we look at a statue or a photograph, we realize that they only *represent* reality; they are not reality in any strict sense.

But this blessing—this beatitude—is pronounced upon those who thirst for more than the confirmation of the reality of God. It is far more than a philosophical quest for meaning. This is more than hungering or thirsting for God. A desire for God and His presence by itself merely makes us religious or mystics. Yes, nothing is more wonderful than to find Him. But we are to also hunger and thirst for His righteousness. Doing this will make us partakers of God's own character as we struggle to be like Him in the world. This is really about our spiritual condition and our journey to connect with our Creator.

In the introduction to this book, I proposed the concept of looking at the eight blessings of Matthew 5 as a progression. The first three express the need to acknowledge our dependence on God. First, we realize that our human spirit can flourish only as a result of accepting our spiritual poverty. We become aware of our perpetual loss, the pain arising from the sin that separates us from our Creator. And we begin to grasp that the way of salvation is of heavenly construction, that our efforts are nothing compared to the rescue operation effected at Calvary and supported by Christ's activity in heaven's sanctuary.

Could it be that the Sermon on the Mount is commencing with an abbreviated outline of the believer's spiritual experience? That our journey must head downward toward a ground zero of total need before it can truly grow in power and fulfillment of God's plan for our lives?

If the Beatitudes can be seen as a spiritual progression, then this one is paradoxically both the lowest and the highest point in our journey. It is the lowest because we are facing a need that cannot go unfulfilled. The object of this deepest of desires is righteousness, which can well represent every other spiritual blessing. We are to "seek first his kingdom and his righteousness, and all these things will be given to [us]" (Matthew 6:33). We hunger and thirst after Christ's righteousness because our own righteousness is more like "filthy rags" (Isaiah 64:6). His righteousness makes it possible for us to receive God's blessings. It is also the highest point in our experience because it places us on the path to untold spiritual riches.

Why describe this spiritual condition in terms of thirst and hunger? Allow me to offer a couple of reasons. First, there's nothing like thirst and hunger to concentrate our attention. They may be ignored for a while, but eventually, either they are satisfied or death occurs. It's that simple; either we eat and drink or we die. Every other consideration falls by the wayside. Every ambition, sense of pride, or propriety must give way to this need. This is a spiritual cul de sac, the bottom of the barrel, the ICU of the soul.

Most of us living in affluent societies have a hard time understanding what real thirst and hunger look like. We have never seen parents preparing patties of animal fat and dirt to feed to their children or nursing babies with sugar water; we haven't seen young kids scouring the city dumps for scraps of food. We don't know much about parched lips and the pain of empty stomachs that eventually stop producing gastric acid.

Our spiritual need for God's righteousness is this dire. David knew the depths of this need. As he daily lived the challenges of hiding from Saul in the Judean desert, he cried:

> You, God, are my God,
>   earnestly I seek you;
> I thirst for you,
>   my whole being longs for you,
> in a dry and parched land
>   where there is no water (Psalm 63:1).

This understanding sharpened his senses and gave him an ultimate purpose: "My soul thirsts for God, for the living God. When can I go and meet with God?" (Psalm 42:2).

In a previous chapter, we mentioned teachable moments. Educators and influencers learn to recognize or create these opportunities. The term refers to a particular moment in a person's journey when events or conditions facilitate a state of mind conducive to learning. In the case of David, Nathan the prophet masterfully creates a teachable moment by way of a story that speaks to David's emotions and sense of fairness. Nathan tells David about a powerful man who takes another man's only possession, his prized lamb, and prepares it for his guest. As David's anger is awakened against this act of injustice, Nathan hits him with a powerful intervention. "You are the man!" Nathan says and then goes on to list David's not-so-secret sins (see 2 Samuel 12:1–15).

This profound recognition of his guilt brings David to his knees. Psalm 51 is a public acknowledgment of his sin, an everlasting showcase of true repentance and the seeking of forgiveness. We are still moved by the pouring out of David's heart in prayer:

> Have mercy on me, O God,
>   according to your unfailing love;
> according to your great compassion
>   blot out my transgressions.
> Wash away all my iniquity
>   and cleanse me from my sin.
>
> For I know my transgressions,
>   and my sin is always before me.
> Against you, you only, have I sinned
>   and done what is evil in your sight;
> so you are right in your verdict
>   and justified when you judge.
> Surely I was sinful at birth,
>   sinful from the time my mother conceived me.
> Yet you desired faithfulness even in the womb;
>   you taught me wisdom in that secret place.
>
> Cleanse me with hyssop, and I will be clean;
>   wash me, and I will be whiter than snow.
> Let me hear joy and gladness;

let the bones you have crushed rejoice.
Hide your face from my sins
	and blot out all my iniquity.

Create in me a pure heart, O God,
	and renew a steadfast spirit within me.
Do not cast me from your presence
	or take your Holy Spirit from me.
Restore to me the joy of your salvation
	and grant me a willing spirit, to sustain me (verses 1–12).

How powerful and soul cleansing are these words and the interaction they represent! They speak of a pure and utter recognition of the human need and complete faith in God's mercy and power. They speak to a deep knowledge of God's character and an open recognition of our own evil. There are no excuses here, no situational ethics, no transfer of blame. "I know my transgressions." "I have sinned and done evil." "Cleanse me." "Wash me." "Blot out my iniquities." "Create in me a pure heart."

This is what hungering and thirsting after God's righteousness looks like. If we were to represent this physically, the position of our bodies would be lower than when we are on our knees. It would look more like lying prostrate on the ground, face down, arms extended from our sides. We wouldn't be able to go any lower without going underground.

Thirst and hunger also hint at the need for constant spiritual renewal. These are appetites that are not satisfied permanently. They return day after day or in a matter of hours. One great meal is not enough. We need new pardons and daily supplies of God's grace. Manna must fall again and again. God's living water must keep flowing into our lives time after time. The human soul calls for regular meals of Christ's righteousness, grace to face the work of each day.

Spiritual thirst and hunger come from a deep sense of our own emptiness. Much has been said about the fact that God has a plan for our lives, that He wants to use every one of us to fulfill His purpose. But the Lord cannot use us unless we recognize our emptiness. We talk about giving everything to Jesus. But even when we give everything, we do not give much. Without Jesus, we are empty. We have nothing. All we have we owe to Him. We have nothing that He needs.

When we feel important and valuable, God cannot fill us or use us as He wishes. We must become like empty jars. What we bring to Him is a life of sin and rebellion, of mistakes, frustrations, and misconceptions. But Jesus takes this empty jar and transforms it to His honor and glory. Only He can make our life and talents truly valuable. He fills "the hungry with good things" (Luke 1:53); He "will refresh the weary and satisfy the faint" (Jeremiah 31:25).

Only He can satisfy our hunger and thirst for righteousness because He is the one who "set eternity" into our minds (Ecclesiastes 3:11). Saint Augustine wrote in the Middle Ages: "You have made us for yourself, and our heart is restless until it rests in you."[1] Since God sets eternity in our hearts, we have an undying longing for permanence and meaning. We try to satisfy it with material things, the pursuit of pleasure, status, financial success, sexual conquests, mind-altering drugs, professional excellence, and the exercise of religious disciplines. But the longing remains. Isaiah described it in these words:

"Why spend money on what is not bread,
   and your labor on what does not satisfy?
Listen, listen to me, and eat what is good,
   and you will delight in the richest of fare.
Give ear and come to me;
   listen, that you may live" (Isaiah 55:2, 3).

Jeremiah also expressed the futility of trying to satisfy this deepest of longings with human remedies:

"My people [God says] have committed two sins:

They have forsaken me,
    the spring of living water,
and have dug their own cisterns,
    broken cisterns that cannot hold water" (Jeremiah 2:13).

Sometimes we believers are lost inside the Father's house. We know the Spirit is beckoning us to a deeper experience, but we keep turning away to the game of religion, of superficial busyness and artificial piety. We may not attempt to satisfy our insatiable hunger and thirst for spiritual fullness with the temporary pleasures of this world, but we remain empty all the same.

Let's hear what Jesus is saying here. First, He is telling us that being thirsty and hungry for righteousness is not only acceptable but also, in fact, a condition for being blessed, a desirable state of being. Second, He is promising that this relentless emptiness, when properly acknowledged, will be satisfied.

The Beatitudes may be seen as a song about emptiness and fullness. The first four (Matthew 5:1–6) express the believer's journey toward fullness and good. Verses 7–10 show what spiritual fullness looks like, and it is explained through the concept of righteousness. Righteousness manifests itself in the life of those who are spiritually full.

What is this righteousness? In very simple terms, righteousness can be seen as "doing what's right." It is prominent in the rest of Sermon on the Mount, mentioned in verses 6, 10, and 20, as well as in verses 1 and 33 of Matthew 6. Its first occurrence after this beatitude tells us that God's blessing is upon those who are persecuted for "righteousness' sake" (Matthew 5:10, KJV).

The way of the Beatitudes is a search for a spiritual condition that, when achieved, leads to persecution. What does this mean? It means that the satisfaction of our spiritual emptiness produces a state of opposition to the world. Why? Because spiritual fullness is offensive to sinful human nature. Let's see how later uses of the word in the Sermon on the Mount describe the concept of righteousness as a result of achieving spiritual fullness.

In verse 20, Jesus says, "I tell you that unless your righteousness surpasses that of the Pharisees and the teachers of the law, you will certainly not enter the kingdom of heaven." Then He goes on to illustrate what He means by referring to the observance of the Ten Commandments.

Spiritual fullness dictates that not only do we not kill, but we also must not live in anger against others because hating is a way of "killing" in our hearts (verses 21–26).

In verses 27–30, Jesus shows that keeping the seventh commandment is about more than acting on a lustful desire; it is also about cherishing impure thoughts.

We are challenged to do better than what the rules allow. The fact that divorce is an option does not grant us a license to be unloving and harsh in our family relationships (verses 31, 32).

In verses 33–37, we are told to keep our oaths and to be so trustworthy that we do not need oaths to move us to do what is right.

In verses 38–42, righteousness means that we should come to the place where we don't obsess over retribution and ego-saving defensiveness but have become "big" enough to turn the other cheek and return good for evil.

We are told that we are not to follow the law of the jungle, where we love our fellow lions and tigers but prey on the rest. We are to love not only the members of our tribe, our family, or faith but also our enemies, and we are to pray for those who persecute us.

It should be obvious by now why this condition produces persecution. Being full of Christ is a refusal of everything the world offers. This difference marks us and, in specific circumstances, will provoke the ire of those who do not understand our quest for God's righteousness.

But this condition of utter spiritual need also serves to protect us from the misplaced yearning for things that cannot satisfy. This hunger and thirst for God's righteousness is His way of reminding us that we were made for another world, another time, and another place.

What we pursue in this life is the measure of what really interests us. Let us make God's righteousness the central pursuit of our lives. Just as we aspire to satisfy our physical cravings, we have a choice as to our spiritual diet. Let us pray that we will come to estimate everything in this world as a loss in contrast with the matchless beauty of our wonderful Savior.

Application
Will we ever achieve spiritual fullness in this life? (Philippians 3:12–14)

A prayer for spiritual nourishment
My God, I understand my complete need of Your righteousness. It hurts to acknowledge my emptiness, but my heart can stay full of You only temporarily. Sometimes I feel satisfied, inundated with joy and hope, but life has a way of perforating my spiritual vessel and bringing me to my reserves. If I may use a modern analogy, I'm like an electric car that constantly needs recharging, and You are my charging station. In fact, I can't, and shouldn't, disconnect from You without peril. There is no substitute for You, and I know this deep in my soul.

What we might include in a prayer for spiritual nourishment
- Declaring our specific need for spiritual food
- Asking for the full presence of the Holy Spirit in our life
- Reviewing our life priorities and what they reveal about our hearts

---

1. Augustine, *The Confessions of St. Augustine*, trans. John K. Ryan (New York: Doubleday, 1960), 1.

Mercy is a matter of the heart, and it grows as we live in connection to God's heart. Remember how Jesus prayed on the cross? "Father, forgive them, for they do not know what they are doing" (Luke 23:34). That is what God's heart is like. Forgiveness is His ultimate gift to us. Mercy is meant to be passed on as a conditioned reflex from having received mercy ourselves.

—p. 69

Chapter 7

Mercy, a Matter of the Heart

"Blessed are the merciful,
for they will be shown mercy."
—Matthew 5:7

There is one incident during my early days of ministry I cannot forget. Of course, I realize my mind picture is not entirely accurate, but the feelings evoked that day are still with me. It happened in a small town in the northeastern region of Puerto Rico, probably in Vega Baja, where I served as a Bible worker for the conference evangelist. My newlywed wife and I walked to a bank to deposit the small monthly salary I received as a twenty-two-year-old ministerial intern. There, outside the bank, a beggar was set up strategically to collect a portion of the wealth being stored by the bank's patrons. He looked at me with my envelope in hand and made his appeal. With no cash on my way in and with every penny already spoken for, I declined his request.

He would not take no easily, and he had words for me. He raised his voice and said, "Malo, malo, malísimo" (which sounds much sterner in Spanish and roughly translated means "Bad, bad, very bad"), publicly berating me for having a cold and miserly heart. The words still ring in my ears, not only for their public nature and their severity but also because there may have been some truth to them. You see, true mercy is not a natural attribute of human hearts. That Jesus includes it as part of His description of the kingdom mind is both an invitation and a challenge.

The force of the message spoken by Jesus from the hills bordering the Sea of Galilee derives from the deeply spiritual nature of His demands for His followers. To show mercy is a trait of God's kingdom, coming from heaven as a gentle influence on the heart of those who have traveled the road of total dependence on God and are now ready and malleable, responsive to the indications of the Spirit.

To the Jewish mind, mercy referred to two things: "the pardoning of injuries and the . . . giving of money to [the needy]."[1] To have mercy on someone meant to show in practical ways that one cared for the unfortunate. But it is more than the action of forgiving a debt or giving financial help to someone; it is also an attitude of the heart. The Latin word *misericordia,* from which the English word *mercy* is derived, means, literally, "heart pain," from *miseria cordis.* (You will recognize the word *cordis* as the root of the English word *cardiac.*)

Thus, mercy is both a virtue and an emotion. As an emotion, mercy can't be faked. The heart feels pain, or it doesn't. You or I may be able to act out the virtues we aspire to possess; we can show ourselves to be truthful, generous, honest, hardworking, kind, and honest while being inwardly cold and unfeeling. But mercy stands apart as a natural reflex of the loving heart. Perhaps that is why it has such a crucial place in Micah's description of God's fundamental desires for His followers. He wrote:

> He has shown you, O mortal, what is good.
>   And what does the LORD require of you?
> To act justly and to love mercy
>   and to walk humbly with your God (Micah 6:8).

Mercy, a Matter of the Heart

Mercy is a matter of the heart, and it grows as we live in connection to God's heart. Remember how Jesus prayed on the cross? "Father, forgive them, for they do not know what they are doing" (Luke 23:34). That is what God's heart is like. Forgiveness is His ultimate gift to us. Mercy is meant to be passed on as a conditioned reflex from having received mercy ourselves. We forgive our debtors because we have been forgiven. We can forgive a fifty-dollar debt because we have been forgiven much more.

Mercy stems from the cross. Ellen White points to the meaning of Jesus' ultimate sacrifice for us:

> Christ's death proves God's great love for man. It is our pledge of salvation. To remove the cross from the Christian would be like blotting the sun from the sky. The cross brings us near to God, reconciling us to Him. With the relenting compassion of a father's love, Jehovah looks upon the suffering that His Son endured in order to save the race from eternal death, and accepts us in the Beloved.
>
> Without the cross, man could have no union with the Father. On it depends our every hope. From it shines the light of the Saviour's love, and when at the foot of the cross the sinner looks up to the One who died to save him, he may rejoice with fullness of joy, for his sins are pardoned. Kneeling in faith at the cross, he has reached the highest place to which man can attain.[2]

Christ's sacrifice is the vital center of our experience of faith. It is the most powerful expression of the "compassion of a father's love," the basis of our acceptance, and the true prism through which we must interpret our spiritual experience. When life hits us with the randomness of pain, sickness, divorce, parenting challenges, cruel bosses, social injustice, or mental distress, when we wrestle with doubts about God's apparent absence from life's affairs, we must look toward Calvary. Every one of our hopes depends on the cross. It tells us we are loved beyond imagination, pardoned, and redeemed, accepted by grace into the Father's embrace.

The Old Testament was a gradual revelation of God's heart of love. Every lamb slain, every prophecy, every temple ritual was building up to the introduction of God's Son into our history. Justice and mercy were to come into perfect balance at the cross.

God's description of Himself to Moses was, "The LORD, the LORD God, merciful and gracious, longsuffering, and abounding in goodness and truth" (Exodus 34:6, NKJV). Ezekiel mirrored the same sentiment: "As surely as I live, declares the Sovereign LORD, I take no pleasure in the death of the wicked, but rather that they turn from their ways and live. Turn! Turn from your evil ways! Why will you die, people of Israel?" (Ezekiel 33:11). God "wants all people to be saved and to come to a knowledge of the truth" (1 Timothy 2:4). Peter wrote, "The Lord is not slow in keeping his promise, as some understand slowness. Instead, he is patient with you, not wanting anyone to perish, but everyone to come to repentance" (2 Peter 3:9).

When Peter asked how many times we should forgive the same offense, Jesus shared what He does (Matthew 18:21, 22). Jesus did not mean to say that seventy times seven was the magic figure beyond which pardon is not required nor granted. In His use of hyperbole, Jesus told us that grace is as infinite as God's love. We would prefer to have numbers to limit the extent of our mercy. We want to know when we can go back to being unforgiving and mean. Seven times (Peter's own suggestion) sounds about right, doesn't it? We can keep records just as the police do when they add points to our licenses. Go beyond that threshold, and you lose your license; grace goes only this far. Now you are in for it, buddy!

On the other hand, please note that mercy is not contrary to justice. There are occasions when justice must be paid its dues, both socially and spiritually. However, God does not exact justice by providing an infinite number of rules; He changes our hearts and minds to make us into persons who are in tune with Him, attentive to His Word and His Spirit's guidance.

We may need to discipline a child, take a criminal to court, or dismiss an employee. We may need to interrupt a toxic relationship with a friend or relative, but even then, God's mercy should show through us. There is to be a mingling of justice and mercy in every area of our lives, just as justice and mercy coexisted at the cross and in heaven. We are to follow the rules but not be guided by empty religious formalism. That is what Jesus condemned when He said, "I desire mercy, not sacrifice" (Matthew 9:13).

Being merciful is rooted in emotion, but it is represented in actions. It is not limited to feeling compassion; it needs to be practiced. The world around us, our immediate environment, is full of opportunities to demonstrate God's mercy—to our children, our spouse, our coworkers, and strangers.

It is true, our humanity limits us. In a certain sense, we are all in need, and sometimes it is difficult for us to feel compassion for others who in some ways may be better off than we are. But God's standard for mercy is higher. To be merciful is to be like God. It is living by the Spirit, not the flesh.

As we come to God in prayer and submission, we are both challenged and empowered to grow in mercy. And if we look for it, we will see mercy played out in lives around us. I remember a man who cared for his mentally ill wife for over forty years after their children had left home. A church leader of some renown, he served faithfully in his ministry to the denomination while being a primary caregiver at home. Others have opened their hearts to adopted children or entered into ministry for the disadvantaged, the imprisoned, and the infirm. Many make patient care their life's function. They live out mercy every day; when they pray, they share in God's heart and partner with Him in His love toward humanity.

The parable of the good Samaritan speaks to the true meaning of mercy and obedience to God's law.

> On one occasion an expert in the law stood up to test Jesus. "Teacher," he asked, "what must I do to inherit eternal life?"
>
> "What is written in the Law?" he replied. "How do you read it?"
>
> He answered, " 'Love the Lord your God with all your heart and with all your soul and with all your strength and with all your mind'; and, 'Love your neighbor as yourself.' "
>
> "You have answered correctly," Jesus replied. "Do this and you will live."
>
> But he wanted to justify himself, so he asked Jesus, "And who is my neighbor?" (Luke 10:25–29).

The religious teacher asked a question common in theological circles of that day. He was seeking rules, a formula to follow in his behavior, that would guarantee his salvation. In essence, he was asking what he must do to find mercy in the judgment. Jesus told him that finding eternal mercy is connected to being merciful to one's neighbor in this life. Jesus drove the point home with a story:

> In reply Jesus said: "A man was going down from Jerusalem to Jericho, when he was attacked by robbers. They stripped him of his clothes, beat him and went away, leaving him half dead. A priest happened to be going down the same road, and when he saw the man, he passed by on the other side.

So too, a Levite, when he came to the place and saw him, passed by on the other side. But a Samaritan, as he traveled, came where the man was; and when he saw him, he took pity on him. He went to him and bandaged his wounds, pouring on oil and wine. Then he put the man on his own donkey, brought him to an inn and took care of him. The next day he took out two denarii and gave them to the innkeeper. 'Look after him,' he said, 'and when I return, I will reimburse you for any extra expense you may have.'

"Which of these three do you think was a neighbor to the man who fell into the hands of robbers?"

The expert in the law replied, "The one who had mercy on him."

Jesus told him, "Go and do likewise" (verses 30–37).

This parable contains many lessons. It delineates the nature of mercy by telling us what it is and what it is not. After a merciless attack by bandits, the traveler is left dying by the side of the road. Two religious leaders pass by. They see the man and choose to avoid him by passing on the other side of the road. This behavior shows what the opposite of mercy looks like. It may not be hateful, mean, or offensive. It is simply choosing to walk on the other side of the road, the safe side, the side of noncommittal, form, and busyness. This is the side of avoidance and willful indifference, the incapacity to feel sorrow over another person's travails.

The Samaritan, a half-Jew with the wrong religious traditions, stops and shows us mercy in several dimensions. First, he sees distress. You could argue that the priest and the Levite did as well. Second, he has compassion; he is sensitive to pain, and his heart is moved by the man's hurt. Third, he responds with action. He is equipped for it with the materials to make ointment and dressings for the wounds. He also has a donkey and money to pay for the wounded man's lodging and doesn't mind spending it. He takes him to an inn. (The Greek word here is *pandocheion*, which refers to a full-service lodging option, "a public house for the reception of strangers,"[3] in contrast to the basic shelter or guest chamber implied by the use of the Greek word *kataluma*.)*

Showing mercy brings benefits. Jesus tells us that the merciful will be shown mercy, that mercy begets mercy. This blessing is both vertical and horizontal. It is about our relationship with God and its intersection with our relationship with others. We are guilty sinners, impure, sad, and condemned to death, yet God showed His mercy by giving His Son to die for us. He is willing to pardon us and save us for eternity. Every day we benefit from this undeserved, extraordinary mercy. When we turn around and show mercy for the needy, the guilty, and the unloved, we are helping to channel God's will upon the earth. Just as the two tablets of the Ten Commandments show us, true devotion to God will produce love for our neighbor.

Ellen White spoke about the connection between love for God and love for those around us:

> Divine love makes its most touching appeals to the heart when it calls upon us to manifest the same tender compassion that Christ manifested. That man only who has unselfish love for his brother has true love for God. The true Christian will not willingly permit the soul in peril and need to go unwarned, uncared for. He will not hold himself aloof from the erring, leaving them to plunge farther into unhappiness and discouragement or to fall on Satan's battleground.

---

* For an explanation of the nativity story, which suggests that Mary and Joseph were denied space in a guest chamber (*kataluma*), not an actual inn, see Mario Seiglie and Tom Robinson, "Was There Really 'No Room in the Inn'?" Beyond Today, November 8, 2012, https://www.ucg.org/the-good-news/was-there-really-no-room-in-the-inn.

Those who have never experienced the tender, winning love of Christ cannot lead others to the fountain of life. His love in the heart is a constraining power, which leads men to reveal Him in the conversation, in the tender, pitiful spirit, in the uplifting of the lives of those with whom they associate. Christian workers who succeed in their efforts must know Christ; and in order to know Him, they must know His love. In heaven their fitness as workers is measured by their ability to love as Christ loved and to work as He worked.[4]

In God's mind, our fitness to work for Him is directly related to our ability to love as He loves. In fact, loving one another is what defines us as Christ's disciples (John 13:34, 35).

The Sermon on the Mount tells us that being merciful brings blessings. This concept is repeated in Matthew 10:42: "If anyone gives even a cup of cold water to one of these little ones who is my disciple, truly I tell you, that person will certainly not lose their reward." Some of this relates to the human reaction to how we are treated.

To the faithful you show yourself faithful,
    to the blameless you show yourself blameless,
to the pure you show yourself pure,
    but to the devious you show yourself shrewd (Psalm 18:25, 26).

In other words, reciprocity comes naturally to the human heart. When we show mercy, there is a higher probability that people will respond in kind.

A merciful heart is a blessed state of mind with immediate and future rewards. The opposite also holds true; the unmerciful, at the very least, are missing the joy of collaborating with God. The parable of the unmerciful debtor (Matthew 18:21–35) shows that the man who was forgiven ten thousand talents yet imprisoned his servant for only a few denarii awoke God's wrath to the point that He rescinded the man's pardon. Obviously, we are not to be merciful out of fear, but grace is to be shared. We have received mercy, but we still need mercy for today and the next day. And if we understand mercy correctly, we know that God expects, encourages, and blesses a merciful spirit.

A day will come when the King will say, "Come, you who are blessed by my Father; take your inheritance, the kingdom prepared for you since the creation of the world. For I was hungry and you gave me something to eat, I was thirsty and you gave me something to drink, I was a stranger and you invited me in" (Matthew 25:34, 35). God's insistence on compassion as a characteristic of the saved overshadows the requirement of any other quality.

The spiritual journey of the Beatitudes produces a certain kind of person—one who is bathed in mercy, who reacts with compassion for the needy, who seeks God for wisdom in dealing with injustice, who opens more doors than he or she closes. Total dependence, total surrender, puts us in a place where God can truly use us, formally and informally, in ministry and at home. We are becoming closer to God's heart; we can live and pray from His perspective, blessing others and receiving the assurance of His care for us.

Application
How can we become merciful in our hearts when we ourselves have been treated mercilessly? (Romans 12:21)

Mercy, a Matter of the Heart

A prayer of the merciful

You have helped me come down this ladder of dependence with a purpose. Your will is not to make me an adoring mystic but to make me Your partner in reconciliation. Please start in me this displacement of energies from my spiritual struggle to survive to a state where the survival of others becomes an integral part of my journey. Please fill my thoughts with the needs of those around me; show me how to soothe their plight; guide me to selfless ministry where my ego dissolves in Your hands as my hands reach out in support of Your children.

What we might include in a prayer for a merciful spirit
- Asking God to search our hearts for selfish motives
- Allowing the Spirit to lead us to those in need of mercy
- Resisting the tendency to perceive ourselves to be in a place where we don't require God's mercy

---

1. "Blessed Are the Merciful for They Will Be Shown Mercy," Veritas, July 21, 2010, https://veritas.community/veritas-community/2010/07/21/blessed-are-the-merciful-for-they-will-be-shown-mercy.

2. Ellen G. White, *The Acts of the Apostles* (Mountain View, CA: Pacific Press®), 209, 210.

3. *The NAS New Testament Greek Lexicon*, s.v. "Pandocheion," Bible Study Tools, https://www.biblestudytools.com/lexicons/greek/nas/pandocheion.html.

4. White, *Acts of the Apostles*, 550, 551.

Jesus declared that the pure in heart should see God. They would recognize him in the person of his Son, who was sent to the world for the salvation of the human race. Their minds, being cleansed and occupied with pure thoughts, would more clearly discover the Creator in the works of his mighty hand, in the things of beauty and magnificence which comprise the universe.

—Ellen G. White, *The Spirit of Prophecy*, vol. 2

Chapter 8

The Sin Problem

"Blessed are the pure in heart,
for they will see God."

—Matthew 5:8

Do you want to see God? It is, perhaps, the dearest hope of our hearts to see the face of Jesus. It's no wonder that one of the best known Christian tunes of recent decades is "I Can Only Imagine," by Bart Millard of the MercyMe Christian rock band.

What will it be to see Jesus? Just thinking about it fills me with emotion. The blessing of a clean heart will make this possible.

There are two parts to this promise—the condition and the result. The condition is purity of heart. What does it mean to be pure in heart? And how is it achieved?

Robert Schuller's book on the Beatitudes emphasizes an interesting combination of humanistic thought with God-centered ideology. He suggests that an impure heart is a heart that harbors any negative emotions that block us from perceiving the presence of God, including worry, anxiety, pressures, and even frustrations. Therefore, the key to having a pure heart is to seek emotional and spiritual health.[1]

I can't fully disagree with the idea that an unhealthy mind has a difficult time grasping the concept of God's magnificent love for His creatures. Sometimes this notion hits us with special poignancy. I can't forget a young man, William, in Salinas, Puerto Rico, who attended our old-fashioned tent meetings. I was the Bible worker in charge of his instruction. It soon became clear to me that William was a troubled soul, a victim of abuse, bullied to no end during childhood, and without much of a support group.

Slowly, haltingly, William sensed that this new message and the welcoming environment of the evangelistic meetings were an opportunity for him. The brooding young man with shabby clothes came regularly and was one of several dozen people baptized at the end of the series. As a new Bible worker, I was delighted to encourage and witness his decision to join the church. After three months, we packed up our white-and-green tent, disassembled the platform and wooden projector screens, and moved on to the next city.

Almost a year later, I heard the terrible news. William's demons caught up to him, and in a horrible moment of madness, he poured gasoline over his own body and burned away his despair, to the dismay of his church family. I know that these are not the stories we like to share; we often conclude the story at baptism and leave the next chapters in limbo. But this level of desperation does exist, and we have to come to grips with the idea that evil and hopelessness sometimes get the upper hand in human hearts, even hearts who have been exposed to Bible truth.

What Dr. Schuller does not do in his book is trace the origin of negative emotions to their spiritual source. Sin is not a popular topic in our enlightened times of post-Freudian psychology, where religion is the purveyor of unhealthy guilt, not a guiding framework for a hopeful life. But sin is the underlying explanation for all the darkness in human existence. God is light. "Every good and perfect gift is from above, coming down from the Father of the heavenly lights, who does not change like shifting shadows" (James 1:17). Sin is the opposite. Isaiah describes the sinful condition in this way:

> So justice is far from us,
>   and righteousness does not reach us.
> We look for light, but all is darkness;
>   for brightness, but we walk in deep shadows.
> Like the blind we grope along the wall,
>   feeling our way like people without eyes.
> At midday we stumble as if it were twilight;
>   among the strong, we are like the dead.
> We all growl like bears;
>   we moan mournfully like doves.
> We look for justice, but find none;
>   for deliverance, but it is far away.
>
> For our offenses are many in your sight,
>   and our sins testify against us (Isaiah 59:9–12).

Sin is darkness and shadows, inability to see, spiritual death, desperation, sadness. It causes injustice and hopelessness. Sin can be washed away only by the blood of the Lamb, who "takes away the sin of the world" (John 1:29). John returns to the theme of light versus darkness in his first epistle:

> This is the message we have heard from him and declare to you: God is light; in him there is no darkness at all. If we claim to have fellowship with him and yet walk in the darkness, we lie and do not live out the truth. But if we walk in the light, as he is in the light, we have fellowship with one another, and the blood of Jesus, his Son, purifies us from all sin. . . .
>   If we confess our sins, he is faithful and just and will

forgive us our sins and purify us from all unrighteousness
(1 John 1:5–9).

The pure in heart are those who have been cleansed by the
blood of Christ. Without this cleansing, no one can see the face
of God. We again remember David's plea when he said: "Create
in me a pure heart, O God, and renew a steadfast spirit within
me" (Psalm 51:10). A pure heart is not optional for the believer
but a condition provided by God to the one who sincerely asks
for it. We want to be clean because we want to see Jesus.

The Old Testament contains numerous allusions to purity in
connection with the sanctuary and its services. The priests had
continual access to a great basin filled with water in the courtyard of the temple, and they ceremonially washed their hands
every time they were to offer a sacrifice. I wonder how many of
those priests resented the constant washing that preceded every
priestly function.

Ellen White talks about the contrast between ceremonial
purity and the need for personal sanctification.

> The Jews were so exacting in regard to ceremonial purity
> that their regulations were extremely burdensome. Their
> minds were so occupied with rules and restrictions, and
> the fear of outward defilement, that they lost sight of the
> necessity for purity of motive and nobility of action. They
> did not perceive the stain that selfishness, injustice, and
> malice, leave upon the soul.[2]

These words are profound in their simplicity. They speak of
our inner feelings toward others because, in essence, sin will
always result in negative relationships with God and our fellow
human beings. The impure heart reeks of selfishness. The egotis-
tical tendencies that begin to manifest themselves in toddlers

grow in childhood and fester throughout our lives. Selfishness gone awry supports injustice against others and allows evil to grow with impunity.

The concept of purity is only one aspect of the spiritual condition of the saved. Purity of heart is part of a larger construct— holiness or life's dedication to God. Those who are pure in heart are those who are in tune with God. This purity of heart cannot exist apart from God. It goes beyond innocence, honesty, or integrity. It is a reflection of commitment to God and His purpose.

In a way, this promise has more than one dimension. Being pure in heart is the *condition* for seeing God, but it may also provide the *ability* to see God. In other words, a clean heart is free from layers of misconceptions, selfish intentions, and sinful disbelief in such a way that it allows us to perceive spiritual realities reserved for minds that are fully in tune with the Divine.

Remember Jesus' words about us needing to be like little children to enter into the kingdom?

It is not lack of experience that makes us like little children; it is the purity of our hearts. Little children are unencumbered by notions and prejudice. They don't project their own sinful perceptions unto others. They are also easily amazed by the wonder that pervades the human experience. Ellen White adds:

> Jesus declared that the pure in heart should see God. They would recognize him in the person of his Son, who was sent to the world for the salvation of the human race. Their minds, being cleansed and occupied with pure thoughts, would more clearly discover the Creator in the works of his mighty hand, in the things of beauty and magnificence which comprise the universe. They would live as in the visible presence of the Almighty, in a world of his creation, during the time that he apportions them here. They would

also see God in the future immortal state, as did Adam when he walked and talked with God in Eden.[3]

The emphasis on a godly life and the fight against sin are sometimes presented as the great objective of the spiritual journey. Some will argue the centrality of a relationship with Jesus as a one-size-fits-all formula for spiritual victory. We have created a false dichotomy of faith versus works that has caused immense strife in Christian circles. Falsehoods inhabit both extremes. An emphasis on grace is sometimes used to cover an immature and ineffective Christian experience. At the other end of the spectrum, a message of faith plus works celebrates human religious achievement at the expense of minimizing our total dependence on the work of the Spirit in our lives.

The great truth of human existence, taught by the sanctuary services in the Old Testament and the supreme sacrifice of Christ in the New, is that we are unable to purify ourselves. We have no human solution for our sins. Our righteousness is like filthy rags (Isaiah 64:6), and our thoughts and actions are contaminated by our selfishness and inability to truly love others.

The beautiful passage in Isaiah 1:18 provides the right emphasis in the pursuit of purity:

> "Come now, let us settle the matter,"
>   says the LORD.
> "Though your sins are like scarlet,
>   they shall be as white as snow;
> though they are red as crimson,
>   they shall be like wool."

God takes the initiative here, as He always does. He extends the invitation, and He offers the solution. Through the God-enabled process of repentance, confession, and forgiveness, the matter is settled. An extraordinary transaction allows the total purification of the tainted fabric of our lives and its transformation into a white robe of righteousness. Our victory does not come from self-discipline, repression, or logic; it comes from a settling of the matter of our sin whereby we lay our impulses at the foot of the cross and cling to God's promise of mercy and forgiveness. Our victory is wrought by His work and, even more significantly, by His presence in our lives.

Philip Yancey quotes the Nobel laureate Francois Mauriac's take on the words of Jesus:

> Impurity separates us from God. The spiritual life obeys laws as verifiable as those of the physical world. . . . Purity is the condition for a higher love—for a possession superior to all possessions: that of God. Yes, this is what is at stake, and nothing less.[4]

The pure in heart are blessed because they will see God. We have seen that this works in more than one way. Purity of heart opens our eyes to God's beauty, and it allows us to grow in intimacy with Him. It is a condition we seek because it is an integral part of our all-important, all-consuming seeking for God Himself. We want to see Jesus; we long to be in His presence. Our hearts were made to be with Him; we will not rest until we rest in Him. What will it be to see Jesus? To fall prostrate before the King of kings? To finally see His loving face? I can only imagine, but this is enough for now.

Application

If purity is the condition for seeing God, how can I ever hope to see Him? (Hebrews 10:21–23)

A prayer for a pure heart

The message of the sanctuary is telling me that I need constant cleansing of my heart, that this is indispensable for salvation and ministry. It also tells me that there is no human remedy for the disease of sin. Please be my doctor; search me and show me my sickness. Clean my wounds. Anoint them with the salve of Your forgiveness. Heal me. Sin hurts and paralyzes, but I want more than relief. I want to be pure because I want to see You. This world is not my home, and nothing here is worth more than being in Your presence in that day.

What we might include in a prayer for a pure heart
- Seeking God's gift of forgiveness
- Asking God for a clearer perception of spiritual realities
- Celebrating the presence of Jesus in everything we experience

---

1. Robert Schuller, *The Be Happy Attitudes* (Waco, TX: Word Books, 1985), 147–164.

2. Ellen G. White, *Spirit of Prophecy*, vol. 2, (Battle Creek, MI: Seventh-day Adventist Publishing Association, 1877), 208.

3. White, 208, 209.

4. Philip Yancey, *The Jesus I Never Knew* (Grand Rapids, MI: Zondervan, 1995), 119.

God's peace is not an end in itself. It inherently

challenges us to become bearers of peace.

It is not a gift to be hoarded. The recipients of

God's peace are called to practice the ministry

of reconciliation with God. To bring to others

the blessing of the peace we have received. To

share the Prince of Peace with those around us.

—p. 90

Chapter 9

What It Means to Follow
the Prince of Peace

"Blessed are the peacemakers,
for they will be called children of God."
—Matthew 5:9

The last of the Beatitudes promises two blessings related to the mission of the believer in the world. The gospel is an instrument of peace—peace between men and peace with God. Isaiah poetically expressed:

> How beautiful on the mountains
>   are the feet of those who bring good news,
> who proclaim peace,
>   who bring good tidings,
>   who proclaim salvation,
> who say to Zion,
>   "Your God reigns!" (Isaiah 52:7).

But this gospel of peace often produces contrary and intense reactions. It may even result in persecution.

Why peacemakers? Why does the spiritual journey modeled by the Beatitudes conclude with a call to become peacemakers? Probably because peace is arguably the greatest of God's gifts to the human spirit. Human existence is so challenging and complex that peace becomes an elusive ideal. Communally, the opposite of peace is war, but individually, the opposite of peace is anger and unrest.

We are in turmoil from the moment we face the world as thinking individuals. We face rejection, correction, and dejection. We find ourselves unwanted and ignored. Life is hard, and relationships are never perfect. Frustrations fester and feed an existential anger we don't understand. Life turns us either despondent or irate. Depressed or fuming.

This natural unrest of the human soul makes for difficult interactions with others. From the home to the halls of government, anger is churned into aggression and war. It's real, and it isn't pretty. It may well be the antithesis of what the Beatitudes are proclaiming, the opposite of God's kingdom and its intent.

The very object of God's blessings is to give us peace—real peace. To have peace is to live in harmony. It is not a reprieve from hostilities. Neither is peace the clandestine cold war of repressed hatred or hypocritical greetings. God wills us to have real peace with Him and with others. Jesus told us: "Peace I leave with you; my peace I give you. I do not give to you as the world gives. Do not let your hearts be troubled and do not be afraid" (John 14:27). This is more than worldly peace. And Jesus wants to give us that peace right now, no matter the circumstances.

God's peace is not an end in itself. It inherently challenges us to become bearers of peace. It is not a gift to be hoarded. The recipients of God's peace are called to practice the ministry of reconciliation with God. To bring to others the blessing of the peace we have received. To share the Prince of Peace with those around us. And the world is in dire need of this peace!

Pastor Felipe Andino tells of when he encountered a young woman sitting on the side of a bridge in Puerto Rico. She was fidgety and biting her nails, her eyes lost in the distance. He and a group of young church members greeted her and shared a brief testimony of their faith. For a moment, she seemed attentive to their words, and Pastor Andino and his group felt gratified by the opportunity to witness. But as they walked away, only a couple of minutes passed before they heard the sound of a body hitting the water. The young woman had jumped to her death, overwhelmed by drug addiction and the loss of her children to a court's decree.

God desires to comfort those who live in such depths of despair. He hopes to reach them before they get to such a state. The sobering question is whether we will be willing to serve as His instruments for peace.

Several years ago, a church family I knew was shaken by the fear of tragedy. Two church members had started an affair. The man was married to an unbelieving wife who had strong suspicions of the relationship and the identity of the "other woman."

One Sabbath morning, the innocent spouse came to the church—not as a sympathizer or a seeker. Her heart was seething with rage and despondency; she had to see for herself the woman who was robbing her of her husband's affections. She was far more than curious; she wanted revenge and came with a .38-caliber revolver in her purse, ready to inflict the ultimate penalty. She would have carried out her plan if she hadn't found a peacemaker sitting on the pew by her.

One of the church members, an unassuming, middle-aged lady of quiet demeanor, noticed the visitor's distress. She barely knew her but sensed something was wrong. She felt compelled to put her arm around her and ask her what was happening. For a moment, the woman looked ahead in silence; then, slowly, tears started flowing down her cheeks. She opened her purse and showed the gun. The church member hugged her closer and quietly told her, "You can't do that."

No one else in the church knew the silent drama being played

91

out in the pew a dozen feet from the sanctuary's main door. The woman of faith held the would-be assassin for long minutes until the Holy Spirit had the opportunity to overcome the runaway emotions, and a tragedy was prevented. In my book, that humble lady was a true hero and an agent of peace.

Peacemakers are urgently needed in our sinful world. God wants to use us in a timely manner to keep evil from happening. He wants us to be ready to step in when possible and avert the expression of hate. He wants to use us before evil has had a chance to convince someone that all hope is gone.

Making peace is acting according to God's nature; that's why peacemakers are called children of God. All of redemption involves a search for peace and reconciliation. The theme of the great controversy is the best explanation for cosmic and human history. We are in the midst of a millennial war that involves all of creation and has convulsed the entire universe. When sin entered into this world, the hostilities between good and evil estranged the Creator from His creatures. Jesus came to reconcile the world with God, and those who believe in Him have received the ministry of reconciliation (2 Corinthians 5:18–20). Peacemaking is the greatest motive behind God's plan of salvation.

There is estrangement in all human relationships. There is social strife between rich and poor; marriages and friendships break down in acrimony; there are racial and ethnic divisions. Violence hurts children and the weak. People hurt for the lack of connections and human affection.

Peace should be not only our purpose but also our element. We ought to breathe peace, love peace, delight in peace. God is a God of peace; Christ is the Prince of Peace; the Spirit brings with Him sweet peace. In a world sorely divided by factions, interests, politics, and social issues, we are called to deal in peace, share peace, and act peacefully.

What It Means to Follow the Prince of Peace

Let's be clear. Aspiring to be a peacemaker does not mean we accept injustice or allow others to commit abuse against us or trample our dignity. But we are to fight these things from the fortress of peace. Christ never intended for His church to be defended by the sword or civil laws. He never intended for His followers to become bigots or persecutors.

His disciples were to seek solace in quiet places, in rest and meditation. They were to surround themselves in an atmosphere of peace in the solitude of gardens and mountains in order to be effective ambassadors of peace in the real world of strife, pain, and upheaval.

Peacemaking is related to the commandment to love our enemies. Reconciliation happens as a result of love. No one is reconciled by hate; no one is brought into the kingdom through violence. The gospel is about healing broken relationships with our heavenly Father and with the human beings around us.

Jim Forest writes of living as the son of communist parents at the height of McCarthyism in the 1950s. His father was arrested in 1952 as an enemy of the nation, labeled a "top Red," and dragged all to the way to the Supreme Court. As a child, Jim became aware that his parents were out of step with society, but he loved them—not for their political views "but for who they were."[1]

When God commands us to love our enemies, He doesn't ask us to stop hating what they stand for or the hurt they have caused us. He asks us to refuse to hate them as persons, to see them as needy human beings like the rest of us. He wants us to love others because that's the only way they can be brought into communion with Him.

Peacemaking occurs on two levels. First, we discover peace when we enter into a relationship with the Prince of Peace, when our hearts have entered into the rest of dependence, the *sabbatismos* of Hebrews 4, the supreme blessing of being saved by grace.

Second, this inner blessing of God's peace becomes the basis of our relationships with others. We value peace and share peace. We strive to see people as God sees them. This reality, this kingdom attribute, allows us to act as mediators on God's behalf. This higher level of peacemaking occurs in partnership with God. This is what Jesus does. He is the great Mediator between God and humankind. He stands between heaven and earth with arms extended to both sides.

And mediation can sometimes be a bloody affair. I remember an incident in my youth when inexperience and naivete led me to intervene in a dangerous confrontation. A couple of my college friends and I traveled across Puerto Rico, a country barely more than one hundred miles long that has nearly nine thousand miles (more than fourteen thousand kilometers) of roads. We stopped for food at a local restaurant with mostly outside seating.

As we got in line to order our food, we witnessed a confrontation between the restaurant owner and his son-in-law that instantly escalated into a fistfight between two very irate and aggressive individuals. Young and foolish as I was, I soon joined others in trying to separate the two men, who by then had bloody faces and fists. When at last I sat down at the table with my friends, my shirt was literally dripping with the blood of the fighters. Far from heroic, I still feel sad at the memory of two men who should have been friends, bonded by common affection, but who chose to hate and harm each other instead.

In a way, every human strife expresses an animosity inbred into our nature by sin. Sin has made us hostile toward each other and toward God. R. C. Sproul proposes that the problem with most unbelievers is not that they don't know God or are indifferent toward Him, but rather, they actually hate Him. That's the result of sin.[2]

Most people refuse to believe in God not for lack of evidence but because they don't want to. Their problem is not intellectual but moral. In this existential tension between God and His creatures, we are to bring peace between the parties. Just as Jesus was the supreme Mediator between God and humanity, we are to become part of His team in procuring godly peace in our relationships with others.

But being a peacemaker can be a thankless job. Every pastor or marriage counselor remembers the couple who broke up despite our best efforts and prayers. We have all witnessed a family, or sometimes a whole community, breaking apart due to seemingly insoluble differences.

Real peace requires effort. It has to overcome the hostility baked into our very beings by sin. This subjugation of hate can come only from repentance, and repentance is never popular. Real peace is not a truce but the eradication of enmity. It is the fruit of forgiveness and divine absolution. Speaking about reconciliation between Jews and Gentiles, Paul pointed to Christ: "For he himself is our peace, who has made the two groups one and has destroyed the barrier, the dividing wall of hostility" (Ephesians 2:14).

In the same chapter, Paul addresses the background that explains and solves this hostility that plagues the human experience. We, who were "dead in transgressions," have been saved by grace. "And God raised us up with Christ and seated us with him in the heavenly realms in Christ Jesus, in order that in the coming ages he might show the incomparable riches of his grace, expressed in his kindness to us in Christ Jesus" (verses 5–7).

This is a wonderful reference to Christ's own resurrection and ascension to heaven. In essence, it is promising us a spiritual experience connected to Christ's own experience, which takes us effectively into "heavenly realms." Participating in this salvation is the foundation of true reconciliation. We are reconciled with God and with one another through the cross (verse 16). We are now fully God's children. In the progression of the Beatitudes, God saves us by His grace and can now share His grace through us.

Being consumed by God's purpose, we become lightning rods for the animosity triggered by sin. The same human beings who hate God despise His children. This has always led to persecution. That is the subject of the next chapter.

Application

1. How is God's peace connected to obedience? (Isaiah 48:18; Job 22:21)

2. What is God's mission for those who are new creatures in Christ? (2 Corinthians 5:17–20)

A prayer for peace

Lord, so many people around me are consumed by negative emotions, and I'm not immune. Please make me an instrument of peace; may I act in such a way that others will want to take a breath and rest a bit in Your presence. May my words and actions inspire others to reconcile with themselves and those around them. Calm the tempest in my heart and allow me to join You in this sacred ministry of bringing healing to people's lives.

What we might include in a prayer for peace

- Asking God to fill us with compassion for others
- Letting the Spirit guide our interactions with others
- Seeking God's peace in our hearts as we intend to represent Him in our sphere of influence

---

1. Jim Forest, *Loving Our Enemies: Reflections on the Hardest Commandment* (Maryknoll, NY: Orbis Books, 2014), 2.

2. From R. C. Sproul, "Blessed Are the Peacemakers," Ligonier Ministries, August 12, 2016, https://www.ligonier.org/blog/blessed-are-peacemakers.

Being persecuted for righteousness' sake is more than standing for the right. In this context, it refers to being connected to Christ to such a level that the "offensiveness" of His claims is attached to His followers. It is being singled out negatively for both what we do and who we are.

—p. 102

Chapter 10

The Price of Being Different

"Blessed are those who are persecuted because of righteousness,
for theirs is the kingdom of heaven."
—Matthew 5:10

In the summer of 2019, my wife and I traveled to Yellowstone National Park with our daughter's family, including our two granddaughters, ages five and nine. One of the reasons for the trip was for them to become certified as "Junior Rangers." They received booklets, stickers, and pins. The oldest one—the one who can read—slowly shared the information with the little one. This went on for a few hours, interspersed with a couple of seminars by rangers. Then, toward the end of the day, we found a visitor center where the brand-new "experts" were interrogated by a young ranger. The older one answered every question with gusto; the younger one nodded and supported her older sister's erudition. We left with the patches that celebrated their efforts.

I should probably add that it took a while to find the testing station, but the search was worth it. Without the test at the end, all previous efforts would have gone unrewarded, unrecognized. The test gave meaning to the learning experience. This educational principle also applies to our spiritual journey. There is no spiritual experience without testing. Faith is purified by trials and suffering, just as gold is freed from contaminants by fire.

Some of our relatives live in Florida, near the coast. They enjoy year-round warm weather, beautiful ocean scenery, refreshing breezes. Some live in tenderly manicured gated communities, with golf-course-quality lawns and water features. This joy is tempered only by hurricane season. Year after year, they endure the alphabetically named storms as they threaten human property and life with their malevolent churning of winds and rain. Year after year, our Florida relatives tell us they wish they could move somewhere else as they remove the storm shutters from their windows sometime in December.

None of us like the storms, the way they rattle us and destroy our security. But they come with the neighborhood. Ocean breezes can turn deadly, and some of life's challenges are supernaturally meant to destroy us.

What is the problem with being a believer? Why would persecution be a part of the Christian experience? Aren't we the salt of the earth? The peacemakers? Why do we get in trouble?

Faith can be offensive. Believers are perceived to be aloof, in control of their lives, dismissive of others who may have made wrong choices. This animosity, this powerful current against us, is both natural and supernatural. The Bible says from the beginning that there is enmity between the serpent and the descendants of the woman, between Satan's seed and God's seed (Genesis 3:15). The great controversy between good and evil is personal, and it involves and drags with it every sentient being in the universe, on one side or the other.

Hebrews 11 carries a subtheme of persecution and suffering of the faithful. Verse 25 refers to Moses and how he "chose to be mistreated along with the people of God rather than to enjoy the fleeting pleasures of sin." Verses 35–38 offer a litany of horrific attacks on men and women of faith in Bible times. "There were others who were tortured, refusing to be released so that they might gain an even better resurrection. Some faced jeers and flogging, and even chains and imprisonment. They were put to death by stoning; they were sawed in two; they were killed by the sword. They went about in sheepskins and goatskins, destitute, persecuted and mistreated—the world was not worthy of them."

John referred to the enmity between good and evil and how it trickled down to the theater of human existence. "Do not be like Cain, who belonged to the evil one and murdered his brother. And why did he murder him? Because his own actions were evil and his brother's were righteous. Do not be surprised, my brothers and sisters, if the world hates you" (1 John 3:12, 13).

When Jesus included the subject of persecution in His principles of spiritual living, He was acknowledging that believers exist in a realm different from the world around them, that their success is measured very differently. They are poor in spirit when the powerful are confident and strong; they are sad and sensitive to human pain when society tells us to hide our weaknesses. They are humble, not proud. They are needy and empty, and this tremendous sense of dependence makes them merciful, prone to peace, loving, and patient. These life principles also make them abhorrent to the enemies of God.

But Jesus does more than point to the natural causes of persecution; He assures His followers that those who are persecuted for aligning themselves with Him will be blessed and that they will partake of the kingdom of heaven. They are blessed in several ways. They are honored by suffering disgrace for His sake (Acts 5:41). They are blessed by the fact that they are doing good, that they are glorifying Christ with their lives. Persecution is also an opportunity for experiencing the evidence of God's presence and His grace at work in our lives (Daniel 3:25; Romans 8:38,

39; 2 Corinthians 1:5). They will be rewarded. Theirs is the kingdom of heaven.

Being persecuted for righteousness' sake is more than standing for the right. In this context, it refers to being connected to Christ to such a level that the "offensiveness" of His claims is attached to His followers. It is being singled out negatively for both what we do and who we are.

This promise appears at the end of the list of characteristics of the kingdom life. Remember the premise that there is a progression in the blessings of Matthew 5. The believer is shown moving down a ladder of faith and dependence, starting by acknowledging their spiritual poverty, their pain as a sinner, and their utter need for God's presence. Then, once they reach the lowest rung of hunger and thirst for righteousness where they have their personal, soul-defining encounter with God, they can project their vertical experience onto their horizontal, human relationships. When their spirit is under the direction of God's Spirit, they are able to show mercy, seek purity of heart, and bring peace to others around them.

Persecution can then be perceived as a result of this progression. Christ is telling His followers what will certainly be a part of their life experience. Paul plainly said: "In fact, everyone who wants to live a godly life in Christ Jesus will be persecuted" (2 Timothy 3:12). But in His sermon on spiritual blessings, Jesus is not only warning us of this fact but also promising us the greatest reward of all: the kingdom of heaven.

The hope of heaven is deeply ingrained in the human psyche. It has been expressed in many forms throughout history and in many traditions: Babel, Shangri-la, the *summum bonum* of the Roman and Greek philosophers, the utopia of Sir Thomas More, and the end-time promises of various messianic cults such as the groups infamously led by Jim Jones and David Koresh.

Whether this hope stays true and pure or devolves into

man-centered ideals, the concept of a better world, of a good and fair society, of ultimate, unfettered happiness and fulfillment strikes a chord in every human heart. In the Bible, this supreme ideal is expressed by the concept of the kingdom of heaven, and those who grow in faith to the point of arousing persecution will have access to it.

What is this kingdom of heaven?

Several definitions apply. The term *kingdom of heaven* is found exclusively in Matthew (thirty-two times), often seemingly synonymous with *kingdom of God*, which appears seventy-two times in the New Testament. It is easy to understand why the Bible refers to God as a sovereign king who rules uncontested over the universe. A kingdom was the most common and visible form of government at that time. But God's reign transcends any form of government.

"The LORD has established his throne in heaven, and his kingdom rules over all" (Psalm 103:19).

In a prophetic outline of history, Daniel declared that "the God of heaven will set up a kingdom that will never be destroyed, nor will it be left to another people. It will crush all those kingdoms and bring them to an end, but it will itself endure forever" (Daniel 2:44).

The Gospel of Matthew gives several characteristics of the kingdom of heaven: (1) It is "at hand" (Matthew 3:2; 4:17, KJV). (2) The righteous will possess it, according to God's promise (Matthew 5:3, 10, 19, 20). (3) It is also available to the Gentiles (Matthew 8:11). (4) The kingdom of heaven includes both the saved and those who only profess the faith, although the latter will be cast out (Matthew 13:24–30, 36–43; 22:1–14). (5) It will grow quickly (Matthew 13:31, 32). (6) It is consistent with a childlike faith (Matthew 19:14). (7) It is difficult to enter (verses 23, 24; 23:13).[1]

Generally speaking, Matthew seems to use the term *kingdom*

of heaven to refer to God's spiritual kingdom revealed fully by the actions and words of Jesus Christ. As such, it is accessible to all who are born again by the power of God's Spirit (John 3:3–5), and only those who are born again can enter it. Paul explained that God's kingdom is "righteousness, peace and joy in the Holy Spirit" (Romans 14:17).

The kingdom of heaven refers to the reality of salvation, available to every person on earth but made effectual only to those who align themselves with God to the point of becoming an object of persecution from His enemies. It also refers to the future establishment of the rule of Christ as the King of kings and Lord of lords (Revelation 19:11–16).

In the Bible, the concept of *kingdom*, as it applies to God's rule, establishes His supreme authority over all of creation and across the entire universe. Therefore, when Jesus promised that those who are persecuted for righteousness' sake will receive the kingdom of heaven, He was referring to a tremendously expansive reward. It says that when we endure persecution here and now, we can be strengthened by the fact that we belong to God's kingdom at present, a spiritual reality of faith and assurance. We can also look forward to an extraordinary reality of future existence in a universe reconquered from Satan by the merits of God's sacrificial Lamb (Revelation 5:12, 13).

At this point in the list of kingdom blessings, Jesus is pointing to two extremes—(1) a faith that has deepened to the point that it challenges the world around the believer, and (2) a reward that encompasses every other promise. The kingdom of heaven is promised to both the poor in spirit and those who are persecuted (Matthew 5:3, 10). Every other blessing is connected to this promise of heaven's spiritual kingdom. God promises comfort to those who mourn, the inheritance of the earth to those who are meek, spiritual fulfillment to those who truly seek God's righteousness, mercy to the merciful, the presence of God to those who are pure in heart, and being children of God to those who promote peace. All of these blessings are wrapped up in experiencing the kingdom of heaven in an ever-deepening walk with Christ that brings us to total dependence, total trust, and total identification with His character.

This promise is about the vindication of God's people. In God's kingdom, the last are the first; the meek, the humble, the seekers, the followers, the peace loving, the rejected, the persecuted will be vindicated. God will be faithful to us. His promises guarantee this. His death and resurrection are incontrovertible proof that He keeps His promises.

Application

1. Jesus promises peace but assures us that we will face persecution. How do we reconcile both concepts? (John 14:27; 16:33)

2. How do we find a blessing in opposition or ostracism? (Romans 8:28; Hebrews 10:36–39)

A prayer of the persecuted

Father, You know that none of us appreciates being mistreated, misunderstood, or persecuted—especially when it comes as a result of doing the "right thing." Thanks for assuring me that partnering with You will ultimately end well. Thanks for allowing me the privilege of being Your follower, and if my resolve is to be tested, please keep me faithful.

What we might include in a prayer of the persecuted
- Asking God to help us see His hand in life's challenges
- Learning to come closer to God as we face trials
- Learning to appreciate the power of hope in coping with adversity

---

1. John F. Walvoord, "The Kingdom of Heaven," Bible.org, January 1, 2008, https://bible.org/article/kingdom-heaven.

We practice an extrinsic religion that is shown in visible, tangible expressions, such as church attendance and religious affiliation. There is also an intrinsic religion, one that perceives God as a vital part of our existence. Moreover, an intrinsic religious experience rests on the supposition that God not only exists but desires to maintain a relationship with His creatures.

—p. 111

Chapter 11

The Science of Spiritual Blessings

For several decades, there has been a renewed interest in the intersection of science and religion. This is different from the philosophical discussion about the two disciplines. Much of it is based on the desire to employ scientific methodology to confirm the claims of religious faith. In principle, I reject the notion of using science as the arbiter of faith. Although science and religion often clash in their implications and the worldviews they support, one can argue that science studies the empirical realm, while religion pertains to the questions of meaning and morality. According to this position, religion and science cannot contradict each other because they inhabit different dimensions.

But you could also argue that science and religion have legitimate overlaps when they attempt to explain certain aspects of reality. Questions of origins fit these criteria, as well as the existence of unexplainable phenomena such as miraculous healings. However, when either science or faith makes inroads into the other, their explanations often become convoluted and even painful. Evolutionary theory builds a good case for progressive change and natural selection within species but fails miserably in explaining the beginning of life. Religion gets muddied when it spiritualizes mental illness and automatically blames natural catastrophes on sinful lifestyles.

Basic questions should be asked of both. The religious would do well to respect the solidity of the scientific method, and the scientists should be willing to consider the possibility of a religious explanation for the origins of life and the supernatural. It is also true that there is much to be learned by inhabiting the overlap between science and faith. Let us consider this field of the study of science and religion for a moment.

For a believer, the proof of God's blessings is abundant. We find God's prints in nature, in a beautiful sunrise, the complexity of living organisms, and the vastness of the universe. We also find Him in Scripture, in thoughtful meditation, and the powerful sense of His presence. Attempting to measure any aspect of the religious experience in a scientifically valid way can be tricky. Sometimes numbers are employed within a scale to ascertain a person's attitude toward a practice or concept. Emotions are graded and perceptions are surveyed, but sometimes having a religious faith actually produces hard facts. Here are some findings from some of these scientific studies on the impact of religion.

- A carefully constructed telephone survey of Illinois residents showed that the stronger a person's religious belief, the lower the level of psychological distress. This applied to persons in all levels of disadvantage or suffering. For instance, poverty and poor health did not seem to lessen religious belief.[1]
- A study of 1,650 subjects showed that people (both men and women) who were religious in their teens had higher overall well-being and community and marital satisfaction as adults.[2]

- Spiritual support has been shown to be inversely related to depression and positively related to self-esteem in adults facing high stress levels.[3]
- In a study of 586 members of Christian churches, it was shown that using faith in dealing with significant negative events such as losses, threatening events, and disease correlates with positive outcomes.[4]
- The *Handbook of Science and Religion*, which reports the findings of 1,200 studies, includes the following results:
  - "Hospitalized people who never attended church have an average stay of three times longer than people who attend regularly.
  - "Heart patients were 14 times more likely to die following surgery if they did not participate in a religion.
  - "Elderly people who never or rarely attended church had a stroke rate double that of people who attended regularly."[5]

Where do these benefits come from? Do they come from the formal expression of religion? Or do they come from the internal orientation of our beings toward God? Those of us who are religious experience religion in two dimensions. We practice an extrinsic religion that is shown in visible, tangible expressions such as church attendance and religious affiliation. There is also an intrinsic religion, one that perceives God as a vital part of our existence. Moreover, an intrinsic religious experience rests on the supposition that God not only exists but also desires to maintain a relationship with His creatures. As Hebrews 11:6 describes faith, "Anyone who comes to him [God] must believe that he exists and that he rewards those who earnestly seek him."

Another way of referring to the extrinsic and intrinsic dimensions of our spiritual experience is by thinking of our public persona and our internal persona—our truest identity. Our external persona tells those around us how we want to be perceived, our practices, our traditions, our appearance, our status. The internal persona lives within the confines of our minds and hearts and is fully known only by God and ourselves—when we practice healthy introspection. By the way, the closer those two identities are to each other, the healthier we are as individuals. Discrepancies between our public persona and our internal identity can lead only to anguish and psychological distress.

True, efficacious religion makes God the center of all things, the source of all spiritual blessings. Let's go back to the Sermon of the Mount for a minute and attempt to see the initial list of blessings from a different angle.

"Blessed are the poor in spirit,
    for theirs is the kingdom of heaven.
Blessed are those who mourn,
    for they will be comforted.
Blessed are the meek,
    for they will inherit the earth.
Blessed are those who hunger and thirst for righteousness,
    for they will be filled.
Blessed are the merciful,
    for they will be shown mercy.
Blessed are the pure in heart,
    for they will see God.
Blessed are the peacemakers,
    for they will be called children of God.
Blessed are those who are persecuted because of righteousness,
    for theirs is the kingdom of heaven" (Matthew 5:3–10).

Here is the point: none of this, nothing in this list, is about human achievement. Human-centered religion is not effectual. Human-centered religion may seem reasonable. It may be principled, attractive, and even rewarding. But human-centered religion, whether it is practiced in the confines of the heart or from the pews of organized churches, is closer to atheism than to a condition of spiritual blessedness.

Let me propose that the blessings of Matthew 5 are not a list of characteristics that produce a result. Being poor in spirit does not make you deserve the kingdom of heaven. You don't receive the earth as your inheritance as a consequence of being meek. You are not shown mercy because you are merciful. These are not cause-and-effect dictums. I think that every one of these statements is about God and how He wants our lives to be blessed. A Spirit-led life, a spiritual life, reflects God's own character of love. A growing connection with God will bring a state of blessedness that includes the gifts of participation in God's kingdom, God's comforting presence, a glorious future, spiritual fulfillment, God's mercy, the promise of His presence, having God as our Father.

It's all about Him. When we engage with Him in prayer, seek Him in our devotions, and ask Him to bless us, we are displacing the vital center of our identity from us to Him. We are telling Him we can't live without Him. He is more important to us than life itself. He is our center, the axis of our existence.

Remember Copernicus? Nicolaus Copernicus (1473–1543) was a Prussian scholar who spoke several languages and was proficient in astronomy, mathematics, and medicine. In 1514 he published his *Comentariolus* (brief commentary) on the movements of the planets in the solar system. His second, more serious book on the topic, titled *De revolutionibus orbium coelestium* (About the revolutions of the celestial bodies), was published just before his death, several years after he wrote it. It forever transformed the study of astronomy by proposing that the sun, not the earth, was at the center of the system and that planets revolved around the sun in circular orbits.

Opposition to Copernicus came from various quarters. Astronomers, mathematicians, and theologians spoke against his ideas, including the Reformer Martin Luther and individuals within the Catholic Church. Luther's associate Andreas Osiander said of Copernicus, "This fool wants to turn the whole art of astronomy upside down."[6]

You see, the accepted model of the universe, crafted by Claudius Ptolemy in the second century, called for the earth as the center of the universe, with the sun and the other planets orbiting around it in circles. This view lasted over a thousand years, in part due to the support of philosophers and church leaders who defended it on the basis of its alignment with religious notions. In fact, Copernicus was so concerned with the religious leaders' reaction to his ideas that he dedicated his volume to Pope Paul III.

When it comes to our practice of spirituality, we may need a revolution of our thoughts no less radical than the Copernican revolution. We may be following a Ptolemaic model of faith that places our own humanity at the center and leaves everything else, including God, at the periphery. We need a God-centered religion, one that challenges and moves us to a condition of utter dependence, complete trust, and deep adoration.

Beyond our acceptance of God's place in our lives, He is to become everything to us, and in fact, this is precisely what He is asking of us. Moving temporarily to the writings of John the beloved, the first and greatest Christian mystic, let us look at the series of "I am . . ." claims Jesus makes through John's inspired words in his Gospel. The first in this series of statements is found in John 4:26, where Jesus tells the Samaritan woman that He is the Messiah. The second appears in John 6:35—"I am the bread of life. Whoever comes to me will never go hungry, and whoever believes in me will never be thirsty."

The disciples seem to be attempting to understand Jesus and His mission by connecting Him to Moses and the Exodus and the manna their ancestors received in the wilderness (verses 30, 31). In reply, Jesus begins to explain how His ministry far transcends that of Moses or any other prophet.

The Science of Spiritual Blessings

The "I am" statements come profusely and powerfully in the next chapters of John.

"I am the light of the world. Whoever follows me will never walk in darkness, but will have the light of life" (John 8:12).

"Before Abraham was born, I am!" (verse 58).

"I am the gate; whoever enters through me will be saved" (John 10:9).

"I am the good shepherd. The good shepherd lays down his life for the sheep" (verse 11).

"I am the good shepherd; I know my sheep and my sheep know me" (verse 14).

"I am the resurrection and the life. The one who believes in me will live, even though they die; and whoever lives by believing in me will never die" (John 11:25, 26).

"I am the way and the truth and the life. No one comes to the Father except through me" (John 14:6).

"I am the vine; you are the branches. If you remain in me and I in you, you will bear much fruit; apart from me you can do nothing" (John 15:5).

These revelations are astounding in every respect. They show Jesus as claiming to be much more than an ordinary human leader. His claims were so pointed and direct that His hearers were faced with the conundrum of either rejecting Him as a deluded megalomaniac or accepting Him as the Lord of their lives. Jesus was clearly saying that He was not just a good man or a righteous leader of men; He was presenting Himself as the one and only Savior of humanity. And we are faced with the same choice.

Either He is the light of the world, or He is not.

Either He is the ever-existing God, or He is not.

Either He is the gate to salvation, or He is not.

He is the Shepherd of our lives, or He is not.

He is the source of eternal life, or He is not.

He is the only way, the only truth that really matters, and the only life that's real, or He is not.

He is our most important connection, the One who gives us purpose and relevance, or He is not. He is our All in all or nothing at all.

We began this chapter by sharing a list of measurable benefits of being a believer. It is good to be a Christian, no doubt about it. But to truly receive all that Jesus is offering, we need to enter into a deeper level of intimacy—a place of spiritual blessedness referenced at the beginning of the Sermon on the Mount, where our human identity is subsumed by the presence of Jesus; where He is at the center, always—not by the power of our will, but by the acknowledgment that we are nothing without Him.

Application

1. Do I need the approval of science to evaluate my spiritual experience? (John 4:48; 6:36; 20:29)

2. How do we know we have reached the point where we recognize that we are nothing without Jesus? (Psalm 42:1; Philippians 4:13; Galatians 2:20)

A prayer for growth

Lord, thanks for meeting me in this magnificent soliloquy of the soul that prayer provides. In this sacred moment of reaching up to You with an open mind and extreme need, I ask that You may consume my very being with a passion for fellowship with You. Please nourish my spirit with small tokens of Your embrace, and may I remain in Your presence throughout my earthly journey. Furthermore, let me see the evidence of Your work in the lives of those around me.

What we might include in a prayer for growth

- Seeking to relate to God with no preconditions, as willing to listen to His voice as to express our own thoughts
- Thanking God for this extraordinary communion between creature and Creator
- Asking God to use us to confirm in others the offer of grace made eternally available by the cross

---

1. Catherine E. Ross, "Religion and Psychological Distress," *Journal for the Scientific Study of Religion* 29, no. 2 (June 1990): 236–245.

2. Fern K. Willits and Donald M. Crider, "Religion and Well-Being: Men and Women in the Middle Years," *Review of Religious Research* 29, no. 3 (March 1988): 281–294.

3. Kenneth L. Maton, "The Stress Buffering Role of Spiritual Support: Cross-Sectional and Prospective Investigations," *Journal for the Scientific Study of Religion* 28, no. 3 (September 1989): 310–323.

4. Kenneth I. Pargament, David S. Ensing, Kathryn Falgout, Hannah Olsen, Barbara Reilly, Kimberly Van Haitsma, and Richard Warren, "God Help Me (I): Religious Coping Efforts as Predictors of the Outcomes to Significant Negative Life Events," *American Journal of Community Psychology* 18, no. 6 (December 1990): 793–824.

5. Jeanie Lerche Davis, "Can Prayer Heal?" WebMD, reviewed March 26, 2004, https://www.webmd.com/balance/features/can-prayer-heal#1.

6. Nola Taylor Redd, "Nicolaus Copernicus Biography: Facts and Discoveries," Space.com, March 20, 2018, https://www.space.com/15684-nicolaus-copernicus.html.

The Lord bids you to come up higher, to

reach a holier standard. You must have an

experience much deeper than you have

yet even thought of having. Many who are

already members of God's great family know

little of what it means to behold His glory,

and to be changed from glory to glory. Many

of you have a twilight perception of Christ's

excellence, and your souls thrill with joy. You

long for a fuller, deeper sense of the Saviour's

love. You are unsatisfied. But do not despair.

Give to Jesus the heart's best and holiest

affections. Treasure every ray of light. Cherish

every desire of the soul after God.

—Ellen G. White, *Testimonies for the Church*, vol. 8

On My Back, Looking Up

Not all personal stories are easy to share. The one I'm about to share is not a happy one nor easy to recall. It happened on August 5, 2018. My wife and I were driving from the site of an ASI (Adventist Services and Industries) convention in Orlando, Florida, to meet some relatives for a late breakfast about twenty miles away.

It was a nice day, the roads were clear, and we were happily looking forward to a time with family. Then the pain started. It localized in my lungs and radiated to the thorax. I kept driving, thinking it was some kind of air bubble trapped somewhere in my back. I asked my wife to hit me with her palmed hand to dislodge it. It didn't work.

I still hoped it would go away, but after fifteen minutes, I knew something was wrong. When we related my symptoms to my wife's sister, who works in the health field, her advice was decisive—go to the nearest emergency room. Still hopeful, I insisted on meeting at the restaurant, where my increasingly pale complexion reinforced her recommendation. We followed her to a small, nearby hospital where, after a few minutes, the nurse gave me the news that the attending physician was somehow fudging. I was showing signs of a heart attack, and I was to be transported via helicopter to a nearby trauma center with a cardiac unit.

My first and only helicopter ride was not what I had ever wished or anticipated. Trauma helicopters are literally air ambulances bristling with medical equipment; half your body rides under the tail section with your shoulders and face extending into the cockpit. You do not see out the windows; you only hear the noises and sense the movements.

The cardiac unit where we landed was designed for a speedy transfer. From the helicopter to the outer doors was just a few yards, and from there to the operating room couldn't have been more than twenty feet. If you have ever complained about having to wait at the doctor's office, you wouldn't be ready for the breakneck speed of heart emergency personnel.

A male technician, a diminutive cardiac nurse, and a surgeon were waiting for me. The tiny lady came to my side and said: "Don't worry, we are going to be all over you." In a matter of minutes, incisions were made, catheters were introduced, and stents were placed in two of my arteries while I watched every move on a screen above the operating table. One artery, famously called the widow-maker, was over 90 percent blocked, and a secondary artery was allowing only 40 percent of its normal flow.

The reason I'm willing to review this scary moment, which, unfortunately, is by no means unique to me, is because of what I learned that day. Beyond the huge gratitude I feel for those anonymous professionals and their expertise, I experienced a degree of helplessness and dependence that I had never experienced before or since. For the first time in my conscious existence, there was not one single thing I could have done to save myself. There was no physical action nor verbal eloquence nor intellectual process I could have employed to help myself. No one asked me to open my mouth, or cough three times, or even remove my clothes. Everything was done for me, outside of my abilities, beyond my possibilities, and entirely intended to save me.

Spiritual analogies are never perfect, but I can't help but think that our relationship with God must reach an equal totality of dependence. Our heart, as in the seat of our emotions, is also terribly frail, assaulted by the urges of sinful human existence. Even when we don't know it, we are totally incapable of making up for our spiritual inadequacy. Our hearts of stone are unable to provide our soul with the oxygenated, arterial substance we need to survive.

Let me develop this theme a bit further, borrowing again from the eternal phrases of the Sermon on the Mount. The virtues extolled by the words of Jesus are the spiritual counterparts of exactly those things that afflict us in our natural condition. He spoke approvingly of the "poor in spirit," the "mournful," the "meek," those who "hunger and thirst for righteousness," the "merciful," the "pure in heart," and the "peacemakers."

These virtues are the products of the spiritual transformation brought about by the Holy Spirit's work in our lives. The natural, unrepentant heart manifests exactly the opposite symptoms: pride instead of the acknowledgment of need, indifference instead of concern, arrogance and self-assurance instead of humility, a false sense of spiritual adequacy instead of spiritual hunger and thirst, selfishness instead of benevolence, unrepentant sinfulness instead of purity, and animosity toward others instead of the promotion of reconciliation.

This is what our natural self is like; this is what submission to carnal human nature looks like. This is where we are when we start our journey toward the light. If the blessings offered by

121

Jesus in His sermon on the mount are to be seen as a progression, or at least as a direction, it is a movement wholly and exclusively actuated by the work of the Spirit.

As tempting as it becomes for us to claim personal success in spiritual matters, salvation will always be by grace, free and dependent on God's initiative. "For it is by grace you have been saved, through faith—and this is not from yourselves, it is the gift of God—not by works, so that no one can boast. For we are God's handiwork, created in Christ Jesus to do good works, which God prepared in advance for us to do" (Ephesians 2:8–10).

The Bible is not a how-to book on salvation. It states the facts regarding the human predicament; it tells us we are mortally wounded by sin (Romans 3:23; 6:23). This condition requires acknowledgment and repentance (Isaiah 1:17–19). We should turn away from a life of evil and selfishness (Ezekiel 33:11). But it does not tell us how to achieve this transformation because this is not something we can achieve.

A paradigm change may be what we need. Christian inspirational literature often evolves into the encouragement of a certain practice or method. Our innate desire to measure up, to succeed, to show results leads us to a behavior-based orientation. Its natural consequence is the sensation that we are contributing to our salvation. There is no lack of Bible metaphors to illustrate the salvation formula. Some of them express the cooperation between the human person and the divine (i.e., the yoke of Matthew 11:28, 29; the cross carrying of Luke 14:26, 27). Others favor the concept of mankind as a more passive object of God's work (the lump or pot of clay of Job 10:9; 33:6; Isaiah 64:8; 2 Corinthians 4:7; the church as a stone building, Ephesians 2:19–22; the vine and the branches of John 15:5–8). But even when we cooperate, we can't produce salvation any more than we can create life out of inanimate matter.

Conclusion: On My Back, Looking Up

This is Christian Faith 101. You can't engineer your own salvation, but you can turn toward God and learn to love Him "with all your heart and with all your soul and with all your mind and with all your strength" (Mark 12:30). We are to seek Him as the All in all, the Anchor of our soul, our blessed Savior and Friend. This is where the Christian disciplines prove their worth, not as a method to work out our salvation but as means of seeking a connection with the Almighty. We pray, we read the Bible, we join the church because doing these things brings us closer to God; it facilitates the activity of the Holy Spirit in our hearts.

The message of the Beatitudes is wonderfully complete in that it makes clear that the purpose of salvation is not limited to connecting us with God. We are saved to become channels of salvation ourselves; our hearts are filled with hope and peace so that we can be champions of hope and peace. We are imbued with spiritual power so that we may be witnesses for God even when persecuted and imperiled.

C. S. Lewis wrote: "We are mirrors whose brightness, if we are bright, is wholly derived from the sun that shines upon us."[1] Let God be the sun that brightens your life. Let that life reflect your conviction that without Him, you are nothing, that He has called and enabled you to walk in the path of blessedness, from despair, to humility, to total dependence, to a life of purpose and eternal hope.

Paul's exhortation to "pray continually" (1 Thessalonians 5:17) is not an abstraction nor hyperbole. We were created to live in God's presence, and the painful hiatus brought about by sin does not negate this deepest need of our souls. This is not religion; this is not our attempt to explain our experience nor a requirement of our belief system. We are nothing without Him, and we shouldn't wait until we face our mortality to surrender our all to Him.

We are not to remain on our backs looking up. In our

weakness, we are made strong, not only to survive but to thrive and inspire others to take up the same journey of faith and submission—never deserving, always grateful, utterly dependent, and deeply loving the One who saves us.

---

1. C. S. Lewis, *The Four Loves* (New York: Harcourt Brace, 1960), 167.

Appendix

Excerpts From *Spirit of Prophecy*, Vol. 2 by Ellen G. White

On the Sermon on the Mount

"Though the disciples were close about him, and his words seemed specially addressed to them, yet they were also designed to reach the hearts and consciences of the mixed crowd there assembled. At every large gathering of this kind, the people still expected that Jesus would make some great display of power in regard to the new kingdom of which he had spoken. The believing Jews looked for him to free them from the yoke of bondage and reinstate them in their ancient glory. But in his sermon on the mount Christ disappointed their hopes of earthly glory. He opened his discourse by stating the principles that should govern his kingdom of divine grace, as contained in the several beatitudes."[1]

On the blessings to the poor in spirit

"In Christ, God has bestowed Heaven's best gift to redeem man, and, as the gift is full and infinite, so is saving grace boundless and all-sufficient. This saying of Christ struck at the very root of the self-righteousness of the Pharisees, who felt themselves already rich in spiritual knowledge, and did not realize their need to learn more. Such characters could have no part in the kingdom of Christ."[2]

On the blessings to those that mourn

"In pronouncing a blessing upon those who mourn, Jesus did not design to teach that there is any virtue in living under a perpetual cloud, nor that selfish sorrow and repining has any merit of itself to remove a single stain of sin. The mourning spoken of by Christ is a godly sorrow for sin, that works repentance unto eternal life. Many grieve when their guilt is discovered, because the result of their evil course has brought them into disagreeable circumstances. It was thus that Esau mourned the sin of despising and selling his birth-right; but it was the unexpected consequences of that sin which caused his grief. So Pharaoh regretted his stubborn defiance of God, when he cried for the plagues to be removed from him; but his heart was unchanged, and he was ready to repeat his crime when tempted. Such mourning is not unto repentance."[3]

On the blessings to the meek

"The difficulties that the Christian encounters may be very much lessened by that meekness of character which hides itself in Christ. Jesus invites all the weary and heavy laden to come unto him who is meek and lowly in heart, that they may find rest. If the Christian possesses the humility of his Master, he will rise above the slights, the rebuffs, and annoyances to which he is daily exposed, and they will cease to cast a gloom over his spirit. That meekness which Jesus blessed, operates amid the scenes of domestic life; it makes the home happy, it provokes no quarrels, gives back no angry answers, but soothes the irritated temper, and diffuses a gentleness which is felt by all within its charmed circle. It calms the inflammable spirit of retaliation, and mirrors forth the character of Christ."[4]

On the blessings to those who hunger and thirst for righteousness

"As the body feels the necessity for temporal food to supply the waste of the system, and preserve the physical strength, so the soul should long for that spiritual nourishment that increases the moral strength, and satisfies the cravings of the mind and heart. As the body is continually receiving the nutriment that sustains life and vigor, so should the soul constantly receive the heavenly food which gives nerve and muscle to spirituality. As the weary traveler eagerly seeks the spring in the desert, and, finding it, quenches his burning thirst with its cool and sparkling water, so should the Christian thirst for and seek the pure water of life, of which Christ is the fountain. There the soul may be satisfied, there the fever born of worldly strife is allayed, and the spirit is forever refreshed."[5]

On the blessings to the merciful

"Here Jesus struck a blow at the arrogance and cruel intolerance of the Jews. Both priests and people were, as a rule, overbearing, quarreling with all who opposed them, severely critical and resentful of any reflection cast upon their own acts. . . . The Saviour desired to teach his followers a lesson of mercy that they should not be wanting in that tender compassion which pities and aids the suffering and erring, and avoids magnifying the faults of others."[6]

On the blessings to the pure in heart

"Jesus declared that the pure in heart should see God. They would recognize him in the person of his Son, who was sent to the world for the salvation of the human race."[7]

On the blessings to the peacemakers

"Our Heavenly Father is a God of peace. When he created man he placed him in an abode of peace and security. All was unity and happiness in the garden of Eden. Those who are partakers of the divine nature will love peace and contentment; they will cultivate the virtues that insure those results. They will seek to allay wrath, to quiet resentment and fault finding, and all the evil passions that foster quarrels and dissensions. The more men unite with the world, and fall into its ways, the less they have of the true elements of peace in their hearts, and the more they are leavened with the bitterness of worldly strife, jealousy, and evil thoughts toward each other, which only needs certain circumstances to develop them into active agents for evil."[8]

On the blessings to the persecuted

"Jesus here shows them that at the very time when they are experiencing great suffering in his cause, they have reason to be glad, and recognize that their afflictions are profitable to them, having an influence to wean their affections from the world and concentrate them upon Heaven. He taught them that their losses and disappointments would result in actual gain, that the severe trials of their faith and patience should be cheerfully accepted, rather than dreaded and avoided. These afflictions were God's agents to refine and fit them for their peculiar work, and would add to the precious reward that awaited them in Heaven."[9]

1. Ellen G. White, *Spirit of Prophecy*, vol. 2 (Battle Creek, MI: Seventh-day Adventist Publishing Association, 1877), 204.
2. White, 205.
3. White, 205.
4. White, 206, 207.
5. White, 207, 208.
6. White, 208.
7. White, 208, 209.
8. White, 209.
9. White, 211, 212.